*If you don't make mistakes,
you're doing it wrong.*

*If you don't correct those mistakes,
you're doing it really wrong.*

*If you can't accept that you're mistaken,
you're not doing it at all.
—Anon.*

TRY THIS!

50 FUN EXPERIMENTS FOR THE MAD SCIENTIST IN YOU

KAREN ROMANO YOUNG

NATIONAL GEOGRAPHIC

WASHINGTON, D.C.

CONTENTS

Please make sure you have the help of a trusted adult when doing these experiments and follow proper safety precautions.

ABOUT THIS BOOK

Writing this book was fun. I got to look for activities and mysteries and projects that I could try—and mess up, and share, and photograph, and laugh over and ooh and aah over—without having to be at a school or a lab. I spent months looking for things to try: this, and that, and the other. Things I had never heard about, things I had heard about and wanted to try, things I had heard about and wondered whether they were for real or bogus.

Then, for three weeks this summer, along with our photographer, Matt Rakola, and 27 kids ages 10 to 15, I worked on experiments and projects, testing them out to see if they pleased us or puzzled us or amazed us or grossed us out as much as I thought they would.

The answer is yes. The microbe experiments (What Died? Grow Your Own Biofilm and Yeast Colony) were actually much more disgusting than anticipated. The explosive ones (Giant Air Cannon/Smoke Rings, Human Slingshot, Soda Bottle Rocket, and others) exceeded our expectations, once we got the hang of them. And the ooh-ahh ones (Highlighted Water, Water Beads, and more) turned out to be ooh-awesome.

But also no. Some of them were fails. There was even one EPIC FAIL that just went on and on and never got resolved until we decided to take our lemons and—well, not literally to make lemonade, but to find something to do with those lemons that made up for all the trouble they caused. (Explore all the Lemon-Lit LED and Potato-Powered LED efforts along the way, or cheat and go straight to Human Slingshot; your call.)

As we explored, we added bonuses and questions and extra information and new connections to maximize your experience and give you ideas of how to take things further. Science is about trial and error, bending the rules, and coming up with new ideas based on what you've found out.

So treat this book as an invitation to play around, make a mess, spring surprises on others. The only rules in this book concern safety. Basically, if you're working with appliances, power tools, chemicals, electricity, or open flames, you need to have an adult there and be sure to take appropriate safety precautions. Be safe, be smart, use your imagination, and if you discover something cool, be sure to tell somebody else.

While some of the activities here don't translate into science fair projects, they do connect with the STEM goals that are so important in our times—not a flower stem, but Science, Technology, Engineering, and Math, which add up to getting more powerful by figuring out how things work and learning how to make and do things.

I've learned a lot by putting this together—including how to make things easier or fix things that go wrong—so check out the GLITCH? and NOTE sections of the experiments.

P.S. Although art is not officially part of the STEM goals, I think art—and making things, and thinking creatively—helps fulfill those goals. Full STEAM (that A is for Art) ahead!

Wishing you good adventures as you try this book.

—Karen Romano Young

Special thanks to our model scientists:

Aaliyah	Jen
Abigail	Justin
Adriana	Lori
Allison	Luke
Ariel	Mae
Bailey	Marco
Brandon	Nick
Caitlyn	Nikitha
Cole	Niyanna
Doug	Patsy
Dylan	Priyanka
Emily	Serenity
Isaac	Sossi
Janelle	Stephanie
Jarrett	Trijon
Jason	Wyatt

PLANTS

t's blooming incredible what you can do with plants: Grow them in weird ways. Figure out what makes them thrive. Explore their relationship with water. Tap into their special powers . . . or eat them.

SEED BOMBS AND SLINGSHOTS
PAGE 12

RAINBOW ROSE
PAGE 10

CABBAGE CHECK
PAGE 15

LEAF CHROMATOGRAPHY
PAGE 17

SEEDS SPROUT IN WATER BEADS
PAGE 24

LEMON-LIT AND POTATO-POWERED LED
PAGE 19

RAINBOW ROSE

Color a white rose in rainbow shades.

CONCEPTS

PLANT STRUCTURES AND PROCESSES

>>> **HOW LONG IT TAKES**
three to four days, including soaking time

>>> **WHAT YOU NEED**
white rosebud
four small glasses or baby food jars of water
small sharp scissors (such as sewing scissors) or a sharp knife
gel food coloring: red, blue, yellow, violet

NOTE ABOUT FOOD COLORING
This works best with the gel food coloring sold at cake supply shops.

What's a xylem? It's the system of cells inside a plant's roots and stem that transports water from ground or vase to the top of the plant. This project lets you discover what sections of the xylem feed what parts of a blossom.

WHAT TO DO

DAY ONE:

1 USE ONE TEASPOON (5 mL) of gel food coloring: red, blue, yellow, and violet or green. Place one color in each glass or jar, and fill with water only enough to create a thick liquid.

2 CUT YOUR ROSE STEM to six to eight inches (15 to 20 cm) below the bud. Split the stem of the rose into four equal portions. Get the split as even as you can, using small sharp scissors or, with adult assistance, a sharp knife.

3 PLACE ONE PIECE of stem in each of the glasses.

DAYS TWO TO FOUR:

4 LET SOAK. Observe the results.

> **GLITCH?** Your rose won't stand up once the stem is split? Aaliyah used a chopstick and a twist-tie to keep her stem vertical, and rubber-banded the jars together to support the chopstick.

> **WHAT TO EXPECT** Your rose should absorb the colored water through the stem into the petals, resulting in a rainbow rose.

WHAT'S GOING ON? Xylem cells in the plant's stem transport water from the source to the bud. Splitting the stem allows you to see which part of the stem corresponds to which petals in the rose. As the rose absorbs water through the xylem, and the bud opens, the petals take up the food coloring from specific parts of the xylem.

If each petal absorbed water from all parts of the xylem, your rose would be a combination of all of the colors, or brown. You can see that some petals do absorb from more than one part of the xylem, because they appear to be a combination of two of the colors, such as green (blue and yellow) or orange (red and yellow).

QUESTION THIS!

• What accounts for different shades of color?

• What happens if you leave the rose in the dye for longer than four days?

• What happens if you do this with a rose that has a natural color?

• Do different roses absorb color in the same pattern?

SEED BOMBS AND SLINGSHOTS

Make 'em, shoot 'em, grow 'em.

CONCEPTS

PLANTING, SEEDS, PROPULSION

HOW LONG IT TAKES
one or two days, including time spent soaking seeds and drying seed bombs

WHAT YOU NEED
several packets of seeds
20-pound (9 kg) bag of soil with a loam or clay component so that it can form a ball
optional: air-dry clay from a craft store can be added to help hold the seed bomb together.
newspaper
optional: compost or peat moss
a baking sheet

Here's a recipe for germination and dissemination. Say what? Make mud pies that provide a growing (germinating) medium for seeds. Then get creative about flinging—or slinging (disseminating)—those seeds out into the environment.

NOTE ABOUT SEEDS
Consider native seeds that grow easily in your area, such as wildflowers. They will grow well and won't do environmental damage or alter feeding habits of native insects and birds.

DAY ONE:

1 COVER OR FILL the baking sheet with newspaper. This is your drying rack.

2 SOAK THE SEEDS in water for one to eight hours. Adding compost or peat moss to this water will make it more nutritious for the seeds.

3 MIX THE SOIL with your hands until it holds together in a ball. (Adding air-dry clay may help.) Make table-tennis–size balls of soil.

4 SET EACH SEED BALL on newspaper and let them dry for several hours or overnight.

DAY TWO:

5 PLANT YOUR SEED BALLS by hand, or throw, catapult, or slingshot them into a plowed or dug-over garden or field.

WHAT TO EXPECT Plants will grow in a random, scattered pattern and won't look like a formal garden.

WHAT'S GOING ON? Seed balls maintain seeds in a good condition for growing. Mixing the seeds with compost, peat moss, and nutritious soil keeps them in a state that fosters healthy plants that may grow more quickly.

QUESTION THIS!

• How would you design an experiment that would test whether seed balls are a beneficial way to plant compared with sowing dry seeds?

• Seed bombs are a quick way to plant seeds in vacant lots or along the highway. Why do you think some people use them for this purpose?

BONUS: SEED BOMB SLINGSHOT

WHAT TO DO

1 USE YOUR PARING knife to carve a light groove an inch from the top of each branch of the Y. This will help your sling stay in place when you attach it.

2 FOR THE SADDLE: Cut a piece of leather or fabric about 3½ inches by 2 inches (8.9 x 5.1 cm). This will be the saddle. (The seed bomb rides in it.) Cut a hole in each end big enough to accommodate the surgical tubing.

3 THREAD ONE PIECE of surgical tubing 1½ inches (3.8 cm) through one hole in the saddle. Double it over and use dental floss to tie it, then wind the floss around the joint about five times and knot it again. Do the same with the other piece of tubing and the other end of the saddle.

4 ATTACH THE FREE end of each piece of tubing to the branches of the Y-stick. Wrap the end around the stick, leaving a tail 1½ inches (3.8 cm) long, and fasten it with the dental floss as you did before. Now do the same with the other branch.

WHAT TO EXPECT You'll have a slingshot with a saddle wide enough to hold a seed bomb. Load a seed bomb into the saddle, pull it back, aim well, and release.

WHAT'S HAPPENING? When you fire a slingshot, pulling back the elastic surgical tubing, the energy of your pull is stored in the elastic fibers and transferred to the seed bomb to release quickly.

GLITCH? If your seed bomb falls apart while it flies out of the slingshot, experiment a little with its consistency. It may need to be dried more to harden it, or wetted again slightly to help it hold together. Consider freezing your seed balls before firing them. You might get them to fly farther, and they'll thaw quickly once they land.

WHAT YOU NEED
a Y-shaped stick. Look for a branch about an inch thick.
two 12-inch (30.5 cm) pieces of surgical tubing
dental floss
leather, upholstery fabric, or denim (your old jeans will work fine)
scissors
a paring knife

NOTE ABOUT Y-STICKS Some people say that microwaving the Y-stick for 30 seconds will toughen it up, but Niyanna and Bailey didn't bother with this. Theirs worked fine without it.

CABBAGE CHECK

Who knew cabbage had special powers?

CONCEPTS

ACIDS AND BASES, PH SCALE
INDICATORS

>>> **HOW LONG IT TAKES**
one hour

WHAT YOU NEED
red cabbage, cut into big chunks
pot to hold the cabbage
water
stove
optional: juicer
three clear glasses or jars
lemon juice or vinegar (acids)
toothpaste or baking soda (sodium
bicarbonate) (bases)
optional: ammonia, other kitchen
substances

What's a pH indicator? The pH scale has acid on one end and base on the other. A pH indicator is a substance that will change colors when combined with something to show whether that something is a base or an acid.

CABBAGE CHECK (CONTINUED)

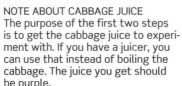

NOTE ABOUT CABBAGE JUICE
The purpose of the first two steps is to get the cabbage juice to experiment with. If you have a juicer, you can use that instead of boiling the cabbage. The juice you get should be purple.

WHAT TO DO

1 PLACE THE CABBAGE in the pot and cover it with water. With adult supervision, heat the pot until the water boils for five minutes. Let cool.

2 DRAIN THE WATER and keep it. Notice the color of the water.

3 DIVIDE THE CABBAGE water into three different glasses or jars.

4 ADD LEMON JUICE or vinegar to one glass. What happens to the color of the water?

5 ADD TOOTHPASTE or baking soda to another glass. What happens to the color of the water?

WHAT TO EXPECT The cabbage water should be purple. Adding acid should turn it red or pink. Adding base or alkali should turn it green.

WHAT'S GOING ON? The coloring in the cabbage juice is a pH indicator, which turns red when it is added to an acid and blue-green when added to a base.

"Fuchsia . . . milky . . . light purple . . . turquoise. . . berry color . . . bubbly . . . neutral . . . forest green."
—Emily

QUESTION THIS!

• What can you add to the leftover cup that might change its color? Isaac and Emily tried some other items found around the kitchen, including soda and peanut butter.

LEAF CHROMA-TOGRAPHY

What color does a leaf leave?

CONCEPTS

CHROMATOGRAPHY, PIGMENTATION,
LABORATORY PROCEDURE

>> **HOW LONG IT TAKES**
one hour

>> **WHAT YOU NEED**
leaves
four clear glasses or jars
four pencils
transparent tape
water
rubbing alcohol
coffee filters (you can also use chromatography paper, available from a science
supply store, but you don't need to)
scissors
coin

What's chromatogra-
phy? It's a set of
lab activities that
separates mix-
tures—in this case,
the pigments that work together to
make the color of a leaf.

NOTE ABOUT LEAVES
It's great to do this in autumn in a location with colorful falling leaves,
but you can also use spinach leaves or other vegetable leaves, and red
maple has a great effect even when the leaves are still green.

LEAF CHROMA-TOGRAPHY
(CONTINUED)

2

3

5

6

WHAT TO DO

1 GATHER leaves.

2 CUT THE COFFEE filter paper into four strips six inches (15 cm) long and one inch (2.5 cm) wide. Cut one end of the strip to a point.

3 PLACE A LEAF on the paper ¼ inch (.64 cm) below the pointed end. Rub a coin over the leaf to scrape it so that its juice goes into the paper. Do this with the three other leaves and strips of paper.

4 TAPE THE UNPOINTED end of each paper strip to the middle of a pencil. Roll the strip around the pencil.

5 POUR ABOUT ¼ inch (.64 cm) of rubbing alcohol into each jar.

6 SET EACH PENCIL across the mouth of a jar. Carefully unroll the paper so that only the point of the strip touches the alcohol.

7 OBSERVE what happens as the alcohol is absorbed up the paper, moving the pigments (substances causing colors) up the paper. It should take 15 minutes or so for the colors to separate. Take the paper out of the alcohol before the pigments reach the top of the paper.

WHAT TO EXPECT Colors will appear on the paper, some in bands of color.

WHAT'S GOING ON? The green of the leaf (chlorophyll) and other pigments such as carotene (orange) or xanthophyll (yellow) may appear.

GLITCH? Jason and Allison advise: Keep an eye on this one, because if you leave it too long, the color may disappear.

QUESTION THIS!

• What pigments do you think you would observe from different kinds of leaves?

• What's the difference between leaves that are changing with autumn and those that are still green?

LEMON-LIT AND POTATO-POWERED LED

We found this one challenging, to say the least.

CONCEPTS

ELECTRICITY, CURRENT, VOLTAGE,
ACIDS, BATTERIES

POTATO-POWERED LED #1:
HOW LONG IT TAKES
twenty minutes (to start with) plus
tinkering time
Note: We spent at least a week on this
in the end.

WHAT YOU NEED
For this experiment:
potatoes
two zinc (galvanized) nails
two pennies
an LED
about a yard of copper wire
paring knife
optional: electrical tape

For the rest of the light/potato/
lemon attempts in this book:
potatoes
lemons
pennies minted before 1982 (they have
copper)
a coil of copper wire
zinc (galvanized) nails
test leads (we ended up using about
30)
an LED
hot pepper sauce
copper wool (like steel wool, but made
from copper)

What is an LED? LED stands for light-emitting diode. An LED contains semi-conducting material and uses electrici-ty to light. LEDs are different from incandescent bulbs with filaments that burn out, in that they light because electrons move through semiconductor material inside them.

LEMON-LIT AND POTATO-POWERED LED

WHAT TO DO

FOR THIS EXPERIMENT:

1 CUT ONE potato in half.

2 WRAP AN 18-INCH (46-cm) piece of wire five or six times around the penny, leaving a tail.

3 USE THE KNIFE to make a slot in each potato that will allow a penny to slide in almost all the way, leaving the tail outside. Insert the pennies into the slots.

4 WIND WIRE AROUND each nail. Push one nail into each potato half, about two inches (5.1 cm) from the penny. Don't let the nail and penny touch.

5 USE THE WIRE from one penny to attach to the nail on the other potato.

6 USE THE WIRE from the other penny and the wire from the other nail to connect to the LED.

7 USE THE WIRE from the nail (the cathode, or negative electrode) to attach to the positive connector (the longer wire) on the LED. To do this, wind or hook the potato wire and the LED wire together.

8 USE THE WIRE from the nail (the anode, or positive electrode) to attach to the negative connector (the shorter wire) on the LED. If you wish, use electrical tape to fasten the connections tightly.

> **FAIL!** The LED didn't light. The Internet says lemons work even better. Let's try them instead.

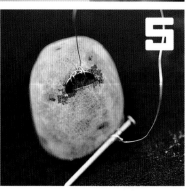

LEMON-LIT LED #2: Rig one lemon, using copper pennies, zinc nails, and copper wire.

WHAT DID WE CHANGE?
1. We used a lemon instead of potato halves. We used it whole, not cutting it in half.

FAIL! The LED still didn't light. Was the wiring the problem? Since we were not trying to assess how well we wired, we were trying to assess if a lemon could light an LED, we decided to revise the plan.

"But it's not working!"
—Aaliyah

For the rest of the attempts, turn the page.

NOTE ABOUT THE LEMON/ POTATO/LED PROJECTS
Warning! Proceed at your own risk. No, it's not dangerous—unless you're worried about going bonkers.

Why? This one doesn't work. Or maybe I should say it wouldn't work, or maybe couldn't work the way we were doing it. The fact is that we ended up trying it all kinds of ways and it just never did work. Epic Fail! Or was it?

POTATO-POWERED LED #2: We used one potato halved, plus test leads instead of copper wire.

WHAT DID WE CHANGE?
1. Emily went back to the potatoes for another try.
2. She got rid of the copper wires wrapped around the pennies and nails and used the alligator clips on the test leads to create the connections instead.

FAIL! Maybe the problem was that the pennies were too dirty. We made a big effort to find pre-1982 pennies, soaked them in hot pepper sauce to remove the oxidation and scrubbed them with copper wool to shine them even more. But maybe the pennies didn't have enough copper in them.

LEMON-LIT LED #2: We used one lemon, with copper wire instead of pennies, and test leads.

WHAT DID WE CHANGE?
Sossi and Trijon went back to the lemons for another try, using the test leads instead.

FAIL! Maybe the whole thing was working just fine, but without a voltmeter, we couldn't check how much voltage we were generating. You can try a voltmeter with your project, but we didn't go that far. We figured we just needed more of a good thing—more lemon power to light our LED. We thought we could do this if we wired together a bunch of lemon or potato "batteries."

POTATO-POWERED LED #3: We used multiple potatoes, linked in series.

WHAT DID WE CHANGE?
1. We tried the potatoes again.
2. We linked a bunch of potatoes in series, using test leads to connect anode (positive electrode: pennies) to cathode (negative electrode: nails), and using the last nail on one end and the last penny on the other end to connect with the LED.

FAIL! Linking in series made it a big battery that should have had lots of voltage, but since it still didn't light the LED, we wondered if we needed to improve how much current we were generating, not just voltage. We tried wiring in such a way that would increase current as well as voltage—linking in parallel as well as in series.

LEMON-LIT LED #3: We used multiple lemons, linked in series and in parallel.

WHAT DID WE CHANGE?
1. We went back to the lemons again.
2. Instead of just linking the lemons in series, we linked them in parallel, too. So each penny had two test leads, one connecting it to the nail on the next lemon, and the other connecting it to the penny on the next lemon. Each nail had two test leads, one connecting it to the penny on the next lemon, and the other connecting it to the nail on the next lemon. The last penny on one end and the last nail on the other end had test leads connecting to the LED.

FAIL! After linking together ten lemons in series and in parallel, and a large number of potato halves, too, we have had enough of this experiment. We've learned some important things about circuitry, wiring, current, and voltage, and we've already learned to distrust some things we see on the Internet. Yes, it could certainly be our mistake. Those lemons and spuds could be chock-full of energy. But we're going to move on, turning our energy to something different: inventing a fun and useful tool for getting rid of all those lemons and potatoes. (See Human Slingshot, page 137.)

SEEDS SPROUT IN WATER BEADS

6

Like watching seeds grow— because you can actually see it happening!

CONCEPTS

SEED GERMINATION, PROPERTIES OF POLYMERS, PRINCIPLES OF WATER

HOW LONG IT TAKES
one to four days, including germination time for the seeds

WHAT YOU NEED
water beads (seed beads or ready-made ones that have already absorbed water)
seeds
water
a shallow container with a clear lid
optional: pointed knife

f you were a seed, where would you want to germinate? If not in a warm pot of soil, why not a bubble of water of your very own?

NOTE ABOUT WATER BEADS
These tiny beads made of acrylic polymer will absorb nearly 100 times their weight in water when soaked, and will become large and gel-like. For more with water beads, see Water Beads (page 77).

NOTE ABOUT SEEDS
Small, flat, and pointy seeds work best for this project. Consider zinnias and marigolds, which germinate easily and are sharp enough to pierce the water beads.

WHAT TO DO

DAY ONE:

1 MAKE WATER BEADS.
Add water to seed beads and let them soak, or use ready-made ones. Place the water beads in a shallow container.

2 USE A SEED or the point of a knife to start a slit in the water bead.

3 INSERT THE SEED as far as you can into the water bead, trying not to split the bead. If you do split it, start over with another bead.

4 PLACE BEADS in the container. Pour water in among the beads, and keep them wet as the seeds germinate.

5 COVER THE CONTAINER with the lid and set it in a bright spot.

DAYS TWO TO FOUR:

6 CHECK your seeds daily to see how they're doing.

> **WHAT TO EXPECT** Your seeds should germinate in three or four days. You can watch the process through the clear water bead.

> **WHAT'S HAPPENING?** The clear polymer feeds water to the seed, which absorbs it and grows in full view. The water bead also acts as an insulator for the seed, helping maximize sun and heat.

BONUS

PLANT YOUR WATER BEADS

What happens?

QUESTION THIS!

• What would happen to the seed if you let the water bead dry out?

"The water beads let you see all the parts of the seed."
—Priyanka

BUGSANDMICROBES

Bugs and microbes are friends. Without them, we'd be up to our necks in dead stuff and disease. Just as with human friends, respect them and keep your sense of humor—and you can get a lot out of your relationship.

CRICKET TRAINING
PAGE 30

BUG AMBULANCE
PAGE 28

WHAT COLORS DO BUTTERFLIES LIKE?
PAGE 32

YEAST COLONY
PAGE 35

GROW YOUR OWN BIOFILM
PAGE 40

WHAT DIED?
PAGE 38

HULA-HOOP OBSERVATION
PAGE 42

BUG AMBULANCE

Good rescue, good riddance, good observation opportunity

CONCEPTS

OBSERVATION, INSECT BEHAVIOR

HOW LONG IT TAKES
a few minutes to one hour

WHAT YOU NEED
a small jar or glass with a wide mouth
a postcard or other stiff cardboard wide enough to cover the mouth of the jar
optional: a sock that will fit over the mouth of the jar; a magnifying lens

You can't keep bugs from flying into the house, but you are fully in charge of your reaction. Will you swat and smash, or sweetly save your bug neighbor? Here's how to do the right thing and get a good look at your new pal.

NOTE ABOUT CATCHING BUGS
You can use the bug ambulance to examine a bug you catch in other ways. What other ways? Here are a few:
• Hang a sheet on a clothesline. Bunch up the bottom and put it in a bucket or jar. This allows bugs to slide down the sheet into the jar. You can also shake the sheet a little to shift the bugs into the jar.
• Use a butterfly net.
• Use a bug vacuum.

WHAT TO DO

1 FIND A BUG on a flat surface such as a sidewalk, screen, or window.

2 APPROACH THE BUG, holding the jar in one hand and the card in the other.

3 PLACE THE JAR, mouth down, over the bug, trapping the bug inside. Hold the jar firmly against the flat surface.

4 CAREFULLY SLIDE the card between the mouth of the jar and the flat surface. Go slowly, allowing the bug to move into the jar or crawl onto the card.

5 HOLDING THE CARD over the mouth of the jar, move to a table. Set the jar down, mouth/card up, to encourage the bug to go to the bottom of the jar.

6 SLOWLY and carefully, stretch the sock across the mouth of the jar, moving the card aside.

> **GLITCH?** If the bug escapes, wait for it to land on a flat surface again and start over.

7 ONCE THE SOCK is covering the mouth of the jar, you can observe your bug while the bug gets plenty of air.

8 USE A MAGNIFYING glass to get a closer look at your bug.

> **WHAT TO EXPECT** The bug ambulance allows you to remove a bug from an outdoor environment so you can observe it. It also allows you to remove a bug from your indoor environment without harming it.

> **WHAT'S GOING ON?** Trapping a bug in this hands-off way allows you to get a closer look, while moving the bug to a better location.

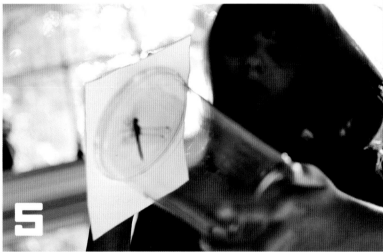

QUESTION THIS!

- Where is your bug going?
- What is it trying to do?
- What is its reaction to being captured in the jar?
- What can you learn about the bug by observing it closely?

OUR TRY
Serenity caught a barn spider (from a floor) and a dragonfly (from a window).

CRICKET TRAINING

Crickets use smell to find fresh or salty water.

CONCEPTS

OPERANT CONDITIONING, POSITIVE REIN-FORCEMENT, INSECT BEHAVIOR

>>> **HOW LONG IT TAKES**
one day

WHAT YOU NEED
crickets (from a pet shop)
cricket house or small aquarium
cricket food
jar lids
cotton balls
cotton swabs (Q-tips)
water
table salt
vanilla extract
peppermint extract
lids from small boxes (such as jewelry boxes)

NOTE ABOUT CRICKETS
Pet shops sell crickets in bags or boxes, usually to be used as food for iguanas or lizards. We found ourselves dealing with some dead crickets, but they didn't bother us too much. We released our crickets, but you can keep yours for the length of their lives (maximum: a month or two), then add them to your compost heap.

W hat's positive rein-forcement? It's a system of training in which the trainer rewards the behavior she wants to see, leading to lasting change.

WHAT TO DO

1 MAKE SALINE WATER by adding a teaspoon (5 mL) of salt to a cup (.25 L) of water.

2 SET UP JAR LIDS as water bowls for crickets. To do this, soak a cotton ball in water and place it in the jar lid. Make two water jars, one with plain water and one with saline water.

3 SET UP TWO box lids. In one, place a cotton swab that has been dipped in vanilla. Beside the cotton swab, place a jar lid with plain water. In the other, place a cotton swab that has been dipped in peppermint. Beside it, place a jar lid with saline water.

4 PLACE ONE BOX LID in the cricket house for ten minutes. Every ten minutes, switch the box tops, in this pattern:
10:00: vanilla/plain water
10:10: peppermint/saline water
10:20: vanilla/plain water
10:30: peppermint/saline water
etc.

5 OBSERVE HOW MANY crickets investigate each box lid, and how they respond.

6 AFTER AN HOUR, take the water out of the box lids. Just leave the cotton swabs soaked in vanilla and peppermint in the box lids. Put the lids at opposite ends of the cricket house.

7 OBSERVE THE behavior of the crickets.

8 AFTER TEN MINUTES, remove the box lids. Does it seem that the crickets have learned to identify the vanilla and peppermint smells? If not, repeat the training for an hour, then test the crickets again.

> **WHAT TO EXPECT** The crickets should connect the vanilla smell with the plain water they prefer. When the water is removed, they should head for the vanilla smell.

> **WHAT'S GOING ON?** Your training uses positive reinforcement—a reward, in this case the plain water—to teach the crickets that vanilla means plain water. You could also say that it uses negative reinforcement—a punishment, in this case the saline water—to teach the crickets that peppermint leads them to something they don't want.

QUESTION THIS!

• Would it make a difference if you switched the saline water to vanilla and the plain water to peppermint?

• How could you design an experiment that proved your answer to the switching question?

• Could you do your experiment with the same crickets that already learned that vanilla means plain water? How would you do it?

"Do crickets bite?"
—Stephanie

The answer is no. The only way they'll bother you is if you dislike the sight of crawling crickets. And ours sang in the evening, which was sweet.

WHAT COLORS DO BUTTERFLIES LIKE?

Make feeders in different colors to test butterflies' preference.

CONCEPTS

VISION, BEHAVIOR MODIFICATION, COLOR DISCRIMINATION, INSECTS, FOOD

> **HOW LONG IT TAKES**
> two to three days

> **WHAT YOU NEED**
> quart (1-L) jar
> three baby food jars
> red, yellow, and white paint
> paintbrush
> nectar (see step 1)
> hammer and nails
> string
> butterflies or a butterfly garden

What's behavior modification? It's a training system based on the reaction or reward the subject gets for behavior.

2a

WHAT TO DO

DAY ONE:

1 MAKE THE NECTAR. With adult assistance, boil four cups (1 L) of water. Add one cup (.25 L) of sugar. Stir and cool. Store it in the jar.

2 BUILD NECTAR feeders as follows.

a. Use one baby food jar for each feeder. Remove the lid and paint the outside of it. Paint one lid red, one yellow, and one white.

b. Use a hammer and nail to poke holes in each lid. The butterflies will feed through these.

c. Fill the jars to the top with the nectar.

d. Screw the lids on tightly, and tie string or wire around the mouths of the jars.

3 HANG THE FEEDERS near one another. Hang them from a tree or a railing, or use bird feeder hooks to attach them to an overhang. Place them in an area where you've seen butterflies—a garden of flowers. Or, if you're using an indoor butterfly enclosure, set the jars at the bottom of the enclosure.

DAYS TWO TO THREE:

4 OBSERVE THE JARS and count the butterflies. Keep track of which jar attracts the most visitors in a chart like the one to the right.

5 AFTER YOU'VE FIGURED out which color feeder the butterflies prefer, take the feeders down. Fill their least favorite jar with nectar and the other two jars with plain water. Does this affect the butterflies' feeder preference?

6 NOW THAT THE butterflies have adjusted again, refill all the feeders with nectar. What happens now?

7 PLACE JUST THE LIDS outside. Without jars, nectar, or water, what do the butterflies visit first?

WHAT TO EXPECT The butterflies should change their behavior depending on the situation. They'll demonstrate whether they prefer one color to others and whether they prefer nectar to plain water.

WHAT'S GOING ON? In step 4, you'll determine whether butterflies can perceive color and whether they have a preference for a certain color or colors. Then in step 5, you'll teach them to ignore their color preference to find the food they want. In step 6, you'll introduce the color factor again. And in step 7, you'll see whether the absence of food has any impact on color preference.

GLITCH? What happens if hummingbirds or bees or other things are attracted to your nectar? Well, why not? Make it part of your observation, and note the number of visitations each feeder gets. Maybe you'll learn that hummingbirds and bees have a preference, too. For more, turn the page.

2b

2c

2d

QUESTION THIS!

• Why would butterflies prefer one color over another?

• Why would butterflies prefer one kind of water over another?

	Yellow	White	Red
all nectar	3	6	8
2 plain, 1 nectar (X)	4 X	5	6
all nectar again	4	0	0
lids only	0	0	0

BONUS:
FEED THE BEES

A variation on this experiment focuses on bees. First figure out what colors your bees prefer by following the same steps you followed for butterflies. Then try testing them using symbols. Use jar lids that are painted white, and use a black permanent marker to draw a symbol on each: a circle, a star, a triangle. Put nectar in one jar—the one in the middle, with the star, say. After bees have figured out where the nectar is, remove the bottom part of the jar, and just hang the lid there. Which lid draws visits from the most bees? Will it still be the one with the star?

> FAIL! In one sense, this experiment didn't work for us. Butterflies have been sparse in my garden this spring and summer—even with a gorgeous new butterfly bush to attract them. We didn't see a single butterfly on our feeders, but we saw a hummingbird and lots of bees. So we switched to the bonus and found that most bees went to the yellow or red jar, not the white one—with or without a star.

YEAST COLONY

Compare the responses of "twin" yeast colonies to different conditions.

CONCEPTS

MICROBES, LABORATORY PROCEDURES

> **HOW LONG IT TAKES**
> two to three days

> **WHAT YOU NEED**
> ¼ teaspoon (1 mL) active baking yeast
> water
> eyedropper
> four agar petri dishes (these are
> shallow plastic or glass petri dishes that
> have a layer of agar, a material that
> yeast and bacteria can live on, available
> from a science supply store)
> two or three beads (these allow you to
> mix the yeast without touching the agar)
> spoon or tweezers
> flat-bottomed jar
> 8- to 12-inch (20- to 30-cm) square of
> velveteen
> rubber band
> optional: magnifying lens, microscope

W hat's a replication? It's a copy. This experiment shows how to replicate a sample of microbes.

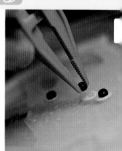

YEAST COLONY (CONTINUED)

WHAT TO DO

DAY ONE:

1 MIX THE YEAST with warm water (about 100°F or 38°C—just slightly above body temperature. It should feel lukewarm to you).

2 USE THE EYEDROPPER to drop three drops of yeast solution in one petri dish of agar.

3 ADD CRAFT BEADS, and swirl the yeast for 30 seconds to mix it.

4 REMOVE THE BEADS carefully with a spoon or tweezers.

5 COVER THE PETRI DISH, and place in a dark spot overnight.

DAY TWO:

6 ATTACH VELVETEEN to the jar bottom with a rubber band, fuzzy side out.

7 UNCOVER THE YEAST culture dish. Gently touch the jar bottom down onto the yeast colonies. Yeast cells will stick to the velveteen when you lift the jar up.

8 NOW TOUCH THE JAR bottom down into the other three petri dishes, just "kissing" the agar. (Don't touch the first dish with the jar again.)

9 THESE THREE PETRI dishes are the replica dishes. Leave one with the first dish (the original yeast colony). This is the control.

10 PLACE THE OTHER two replicas in places with different conditions, such as sunny, dark, or cold areas.

DAY TWO OR THREE:

11 COMPARE your petri dishes after eight hours or longer.

> **WHAT TO EXPECT** Yeast colonies raised in different conditions of light and temperature should appear different.

> **WHAT'S GOING ON?** By replicating the yeast cells, you can see how different conditions affect the cells as they grow and reproduce.

BONUS:
MICROPHOTO

Use your smartphone camera to take a picture through a microscope. Get things lit and focused, then position the camera eye right over the microscope. Works great! (With thanks to Dr. Peter Countway of the Bigelow Laboratory in Maine for the tip.)

QUESTION THIS!

• Why do scientists need to replicate cell groups in the lab?

• What will happen to the yeast colonies if left for another 24 hours?

• What other conditions can you experiment with?

"It's got hair on it!"
—Jason

"That hair is MOVING."
—Allison

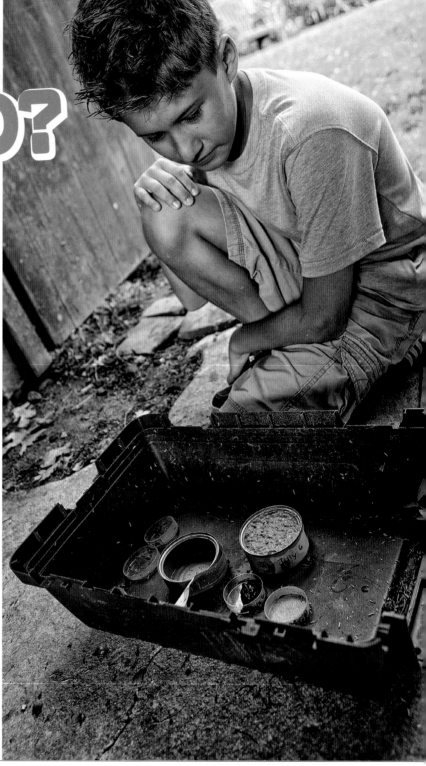

WHAT DIED?

What comes to get food that's left out?

CONCEPTS

DECOMPOSITION, MICROBIOLOGY, DECAY, ORGANIC MATERIALS, BACTERIA, INSECTS, CORPSE FAUNA

HOW LONG IT TAKES
two to four days, possibly longer in cold weather

WHAT YOU NEED
food samples
containers
outdoor thermometer
magnifying lens
dissecting microscope
bug identification guides
optional: camera, smartphone, or video camera

f you leave food out, SOMETHING will come to live on it or lay eggs on it. In this observation, discover what arrives to make the most of your leftovers.

WHAT TO DO

DAY ONE:

1 WORK IN AN OPEN-AIR area, compost heap, or compost bin—a place that is open to bugs but not birds or other animals.

2 SET UP FOUR containers with a small sample of food inside each. If you want, these samples can represent the four food groups: vegetable/fruit, meat/fish, bread/grains, and milk/dairy.

DAYS TWO TO FOUR:

3 KEEP A CAREFUL record of what you observe through your senses. Each day, record the temperature in the area where your samples are. Note whether you can see signs that bugs or other creatures have been attracted to your samples, including any film or mold that forms. You may want to photograph the samples every day to compare them.

4 EVERY ONE OR TWO days (decide which interval you want to study), remove the samples from the containers to examine them with a magnifying lens and microscope. Count, try to identify, and sketch the bugs and other life forms that colonize each sample. Add descriptions to your notes, including sensory observations: texture, color, and smell—but not taste!

WHAT TO EXPECT You may see mold, biofilm or scum, bugs, worms, flies, and so on.

WHAT'S GOING ON? Nature abhors a vacuum. If there is food, something will come to eat it.

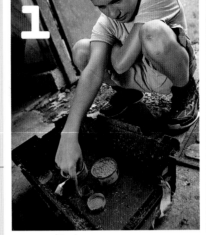

OUR TRY

We put out duplicate food—chicken broth, blackberry jam, and cat food—every other day for six days. We set out the food in the yard, in a cat carrier with a brick on top, but that didn't stop coyotes from pulling it apart and getting the food on the second night. After that we replaced the food and kept the cat carrier in the garage, where flies could still get to it. After we opened it to see what we had and examine it with the microscope, we dumped the cat carrier near the compost heap—and later, we had a glorious infestation of beetles.

"The maggots look like moving white noodles."
—Luke

QUESTION THIS!

- What would happen to this food if nothing were able to reach it?

- What would happen to this food if you let more time pass?

GROW YOUR OWN BIOFILM

Soup + dirt + warmth = biofilm

CONCEPTS

MICROBIAL BIOLOGY, DECOMPOSITION

HOW LONG IT TAKES
three days to one week

WHAT YOU NEED
a cup (.25 L) of soup (low-sodium chicken soup works best)
pinch of dirt
food coloring
water
plastic container
measuring cup

What's biofilm? It's a colony of bacteria that forms on a surface—a pond, a bowl, a boat in the ocean. The bacteria form a thin film, spreading out to make the most of the food source. Biofilm is also known as scum or slime.

NOTE ABOUT BIOFILM
If it smells awful, you've probably met your goal of achieving biofilm.

WHAT TO DO

DAY ONE:

1 POUR A CUP (.25 L) **OF SOUP** into the container and add the dirt.

2 LEAVE THE CONTAINER in a warm place, uncovered, for four to five days. The ideal temperature is 98.6°F (37°C)—body temperature. You may need to leave it out longer if it's cooler.

DAYS TWO AND ON:

3 WATCH FOR A CHANGE in the liquid. When it begins to cloud, biofilm is forming.

LAST DAY:
4 DUMP OUT THE LIQUID
and gently rinse the container with water. No scrubbing. No soap.

5 DRIP THE FOOD coloring
down the inside walls of the container. Swirl it around to coat the bottom and sides. Wait 15 minutes, swirling the color again every few minutes.

6 FILL THE CONTAINER with
water, then dump out the colored water.

7 THE SMALL SPOTS of color
on the walls of the container are the biofilm.

WHAT TO EXPECT The biofilm will form a ring around the container. It will be difficult to rinse it from the container even with soap, water, and some scrubbing.

WHAT'S GOING ON? Bacteria are tiny organisms that live in two ways: motile (moving freely) and sessile (in a group on a surface). Some motile bacteria become sessile, settling down near a food source that can keep them fed even if they quit moving. A biofilm is a colony of bacteria that live on a surface. If you provide bacteria with a food source, a biofilm may form.

The dirt provided the start-up for the biofilm. One teaspoon (5 mL) of dirt can harbor between 100 million and 1 billion bacteria. In the container, bacteria grow best at the boundary of air and liquid.

OUR TRY
It was a hot week, and we put our chicken broth/dirt concoction in an attic closet with no air conditioning. It only took 48 hours for a beautiful biofilm to form. Success! Janelle and Dylan can confirm that it sure had a strong smell.

"Can we get this out of here now? It stinks!"
—Lori

QUESTION THIS!

• What role does the chicken soup play?

• What do biofilms do when they form in liquids in nature?

• Are there other invisible biofilms in liquids around the house?

HULA-HOOP OBSERVATION

Fitness hoops are wider and easier to "hoop."

CONCEPTS

DIMENSIONS, GEOMETRY, MOMENTUM, FORCE, ROTATION AND REVOLUTION

HOW LONG IT TAKES
an hour to make, not much longer to learn

WHAT YOU NEED
for each hoop:
irrigation or other flexible tubing, ¾-inch (2-cm) diameter, about four feet (1.2 meters), 100 to 160 psi (pounds per square inch, a measure of how much pressure the tubing can withstand, but in this case a measure of flexibility) (700-1100 kPa)
¾-inch (2-cm) connector
pipe cutter (it's usually on sale near the tubing)
duct tape
unpopped popcorn to place inside the tube to make a *shh-shh* sound when moved

optional:
gaffer's tape, hockey tape, electrical tape, or other tape in colors to decorate your hoop
hair dryer to warm ends of pipe to allow you to insert the connector
bucket of water to soak pipe ends to allow you to insert the connector

NOTE ABOUT TUBING
You can buy tubing in coils long enough to make a bunch of hoops. We found it in different bright colors as well as black, and did not find that we needed a hair dryer or water to insert the connectors easily.

TO MAKE THE HULA-HOOP:

1 MEASURE the diameter you want for the hoop. This measurement should be the same as your measurement from the ground to your belly button.

2 STRETCH THE TUBING out from the coil into a circle with the designated diameter. You can also calculate the circumference of the circle, using the diameter measurement and this formula:
C (circumference) = D (diameter) x 3.14 (pi)

3 CUT THE TUBING to this measurement, using the pipe cutter. (Adult supervision! It's a sharp tool.)

4 POUR some uncooked popcorn into the tube.

5 USE THE CONNECTOR to connect the two ends of the tubing together. You do this by pushing the ends of the connector into the ends of the tubing. It's supposed to be tight, so you may need to push hard to get the connector into the tubing.

6 SECURE the connection with duct tape.

> **GLITCH?** Can't get the connector to go in? Try warming the ends of the tubing with a hair dryer or soaking them in a bucket of water. KEEP APPLIANCES AWAY FROM WATER!

"I was the Hula-Hoop champion at my school Halloween party, but I've never made my own hoop."
—Allison

HULA-HOOP OBSERVATION (CONTINUED)

7 DECORATE your hoop by winding colored tape around it in a spiral pattern. Add little pieces of tape or stickers to make it fancier.

TO USE THE HULA-HOOP:

8 HOLD IT AROUND your waist. Stand with your feet hip-distance apart or slightly wider, with one foot ahead of the other.

9 DON'T GO WILD swinging your hips. Just shift your weight from one foot to the other, practicing a while to figure out how fast and hard you need to go to keep the hoop up.

WHAT TO EXPECT You may find you don't need as fast an action to keep this hoop circling your waist and that you'll be able to do more tricks.

WHAT'S GOING ON? A heavier hoop—and a larger hoop—takes longer to make a revolution around your waist, which makes them easier to "hoop" than a typical toy-store Hula-Hoop.

QUESTION THIS!

- What's the slowest you can go?

- What's the longest you can hoop for?

- Which way is your hoop going—clockwise or counterclockwise?

- Does your hoop's direction have any connection to whether you're a righty or lefty? How could you find out?

8

7

OUR TRY

One of our models, Jason, was a novice hooper and the other, Allison, was a champion. But even the novice was able to get this hoop up and moving. You can, too.

BONUS:
HOOP OF LIFE

How representative is a hoop-size backyard sample of the whole ecosystem? You may question this observation, but it's what scientists have to do all the time— whether they're sampling the deep ocean, bringing back moon rocks, or looking at blood through a microscope. Choose a spot for your hoop that seems to have a lot happening inside, but be aware that there may be even more (or less!) happening at other places in the ecosystem. You can observe what's in your hoop just once, or repeat at different times of the day— or year. Take notes and photograph or sketch what passes through.

PEOPLEANDOTHERAN

J ust below the surface of everyday life, there lie riddles. Here are a few ways to dig down to the root of some mysteries about ourselves, our pets, and other animals.

SORTING THE TRASH
PAGE 50

DOG BED SOCK I.D.
PAGE 54

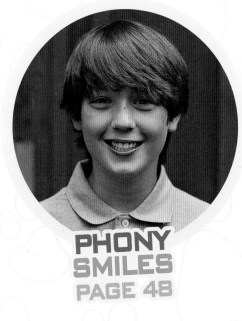

PHONY SMILES
PAGE 48

RIGHTY LEFTY
PAGE 52

CAT IQ TEST
PAGE 58

MAKE FOOTPRINT CASTS
PAGE 63

DOGS AND POINTING
PAGE 56

7·8
Hard boiled

EGG TRICK #1
PAGE 60

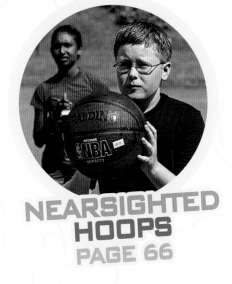

NEARSIGHTED HOOPS
PAGE 66

PHONY SMILES

Smiles: fake or real?

CONCEPTS

INTERPRETATION, OBSERVATION, TECHNOLOGY, BEHAVIOR

HOW LONG IT TAKES
two or more days

WHAT YOU NEED
camera (the one on a smartphone is fine)
computer or computer tablet to show your photographs on
optional: You can also print out photographs and show the prints to your subjects.
three actors
as many subjects as you wish
optional: a partner to film while you interview your subjects

How often do you really smile, and how often do you fake it? Often enough to be able to tell the difference when other people do it? This study lets you see how well people read others.

QUESTION THIS!

• Researchers trying to get better at reading facial expressions sometimes watch video with the sound off. Why would this help?

• Are some people better than others at fake smiles?

• How about those jokes? How can you explain why different people respond to them in different ways? Did your actors agree with you about which joke was funniest?

WHAT TO DO

DAY ONE:

1 PREPARE your photographs. Photograph each actor separately. For each actor, do the following:

a. Select three jokes. Try to find one that is really hilarious, one that's kind of lame, and one that is somewhere in the middle.

b. Take four photographs of each actor, one of his response to each of the three jokes, plus one more. For the last photograph, ask the actor to smile as if he were hearing a hilarious joke.

DAY TWO:

2 YOU'LL HAVE 12 photographs, four for each of your three actors. Show them to your subjects. Ask them to guess real (R) and fake (F) smiles for each actor. The score sheet might look like this when filled in. The response column is for the subject's assessment of the actor's four smiles.

	Actor 1: Wyatt	response	Actor 2: Brandon	response	Actor 3: Niyanna	response
Knock knock joke	Real	F	R	F	F	F
Slide joke	Real	F	F	F	R	F
Elephant joke	Real	R	R	F	R	R
Fake smile	Fake	F	F	R	F	R

> "This is hard! Is a laugh the same as a smile?"
> —Bailey

WHAT TO EXPECT People will probably be pretty good judges of real and fake smiles.

WHAT'S GOING ON? Researchers have learned that a facial expression is actually made up of microexpressions, fleeting glimpses of a subject's true feelings. A still photograph may provide a quick, focused look that clues you in to how genuine each smile is.

OUR JOKES

How does the man in the moon cut his hair? Eclipse it.
Why did the cookie cry? Because his mother was a wafer so long.
Why are all the frogs around here dead? Because they keep croaking.
What happened when the butcher backed into his meat grinder? He got a little behind in his work.*
What did one hat say to the other? You stay here. I'll go on ahead.
What's brown and sticky? A stick.

* Nobody laughed at this joke.

SORTING THE TRASH

What if you didn't take out the trash?

CONCEPTS

TRASH FOOTPRINT, PERSONAL
CONSUMPTION

HOW LONG IT TAKES
two days

WHAT YOU NEED
a kitchen scale
a cloth tote bag
a notebook
optional: camera

Sick of taking out the trash? Maybe the problem isn't taking it out; maybe the trouble is how much goes in. Here's a tip: reduce, reuse, or recycle. What can an individual do? Start by finding out how much trash you send to the dump, then figure out how to dump less.

WHAT TO DO

DAY ONE:

1 FOR ONE WHOLE DAY, throw nothing out. Keep your tote bag with you. Put all your trash in the tote bag. Follow these rules:

a. You can't use the garbage cans at home or school. You can't use public garbage cans. You can't use ANY garbage cans.

b. You can't give garbage to somebody else to throw out for you, flush trash down the toilet, or litter.

c. You CAN recycle, compost, incinerate (with adult help), and donate usable items to charity.

d. You have to keep any trash you generate within five feet (1.5 meters) of you.

2 AT THE END of the day, take everything out of your bag. Weigh it, categorize it, and photograph it.

DAY TWO:

3 REPEAT THIS experiment, using what you learned on Day One.

WHAT TO EXPECT On the second day, you'll produce less trash than the first.

WHAT'S GOING ON? Awareness of where trash comes from can keep you from making choices that lead to trash. Awareness of how trash might be useful can reduce the amount of stuff you throw out.

QUESTION THIS!

• Make a note of each thing you toss. Why did you have it in the first place? Was there a way to cut down on trash with this item?

• Are there common characteristics in most of the items you throw out? For instance, does paper predominate?

• What rules could or should communities make to reduce trash?

BONUS

PENCIL OF POWER

Here's something to do with that soda can you're stuck carrying around.

Stand on a can and it won't collapse. Put light pressure with a pencil point on the side of the can, and it will crumble.

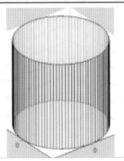

QUESTION Why does this happen? We asked physicist Dr. Todd Baker at the University of Georgia, the professor behind askthephysicist.com.

ANSWER "Imagine the can to be made up of many thin sticks (pictured left); I will suppose there are 100 sticks and your weight is 100 pounds (45.4 kg). Each stick must therefore hold up 1 pound (.5 kg). If the stick is perfectly straight, it is able to support 1 pound, but if it gets the slightest kink in it, it will not and will quickly fold. But that stick is attached to the sticks on either side of it, so if it folds, it will drag its neighbors with it and they will drag theirs and the whole can will fail." Thanks, Dr. Baker!

RIGHTY LEFTY

Which side is dominant?

CONCEPTS

HANDEDNESS, DOMINANCE

HOW LONG IT TAKES
thirty minutes for each subject

WHAT YOU NEED
You'll test your subject in an area that includes
a staircase
a ball
an empty paper towel tube
a picture hanging on the wall
paper
pen
chalk
cup of water
scissors
small box with mystery object inside (your choice)

Babies can show hand dominance even before they're born. Other preferences develop as we grow and change. Nevertheless, you might be surprised at some of the preferences you find in yourself.

1k

WHAT TO DO

1 PLAN YOUR TEST. You'll be testing whether each subject prefers her right or left hand, foot, eye, and ear. You will ask her to do a series of tasks, while observing her to see which hand, foot, eye or ear she uses. So set up the tasks and plan a route for the subject to follow. Here are the tasks:

a. Sit at a table. Take a sip from the cup of water. (Which hand is used to lift the cup to the mouth?)

b. While still at the table, draw a spiral on a sheet of paper. (Which hand is used? In what direction does the spiral's opening face, left or right? This could indicate dominant eye.)

c. While still at the table, look through the paper tube at an object on the wall. (To which eye does the subject raise the tube?)

d. Look at the same object without the tube. Now put one thumb up to block the object. Close one eye, then the other. Can you still see the object with the left eye closed? How about with the right eye closed? (Which eye blocks the object?)

e. Pick up a sheet of paper with a small hole (the size of a penny) cut out of it. Holding the paper at arm's length, look through the hole at the object on the wall. Now bring the paper closer to your face while keeping your eye on the object. (To which eye does the subject bring the hole?)

f. Pick up a small box with a mystery object inside. Hold it to the ear to try to identify what's inside the box. (Which ear does the subject bring the box to?)

g. Whisper to your subject. (Observe which ear she turns toward you or cups to hear what you say.)

h. Stand up. Step on a penny that's been left on the floor. (Which foot is used?)

i. Step over a chalk line on the floor. (Which foot steps over first?)

j. Kick a ball. (Which foot is used?) How about a running kick? (You'll likely take off on the nondominant foot to get the dominant foot in position to kick.)

k. Walk up the stairs. (Which foot steps up first?)

l. Stand with your feet hip-distance apart. Lean forward until you go off balance and put one foot out to keep from falling. (Which foot do you put out?)

Note: Matt, our photographer, suggested we add this last one about falling. And we found something surprising: Most of us put our nondominant foot forward. We wondered if it was like running up to kick a ball—you take off with the nondominant foot in order to get the dominant foot in position to walk forward.

2 CREATE A CHECKLIST to help you with your observations. It might look like this:

Subject	Task	Right	Left
Patsy	a. sip water	X	
	b. draw spiral		X
	c. paper tube	X	

WHAT TO EXPECT Most subjects will show clear preference for one side or the other, but some will be different for hands and feet, and others will use left and right equally.

WHAT'S GOING ON? People have dominant parts of their bodies overall, but also for different tasks. There are different scientific theories for why this is so, but most scientists agree that it has to do with the brain. The brain has two halves, and each half has different functions. In humans, who use language, the half of the brain most associated with language is the left hemisphere. In 70 to 95 percent of humans, the left hemisphere controls language. Since the left hemisphere of the brain controls the right side of the body, most humans are right-dominant, too. Even so, handedness isn't absolute. Some people are completely righties, but may be lefties for sports or may prefer their left eye or ear. Others use left and right almost equally. Others are completely left-dominant.

QUESTION THIS!

• How many subjects would you need to test to replicate the percentage above?

• What can you learn by looking at handedness in individual subjects?

• What can you learn by testing yourself?

DOG BED SOCK I.D.

Can you identify your dog by his smell?

CONCEPTS

DOMESTICATION, BEHAVIOR

HOW LONG IT TAKES
three to four days

WHAT YOU NEED
access to the dog beds of four dogs besides your own
five socks
five quart-size (liter-size) Ziploc bags, labeled 1 to 5
permanent marker or stick-on labels

Some senses get more attention than others. Sure you know your dog—or your brother—by looks. You can probably identify either one by the sound of his voice, too. But what about smell? Try this with dogs, cats, or people. (We show the dog test here!)

WHAT TO DO

1 FIRST, GET THE cooperation of four dog owners. They will need to help prepare the experiment and act as subjects.

2 EACH HUMAN SUBJECT gets one clean sock and Ziploc bag. She places the sock in her dog's bed, leaving it there for 48 hours—two days and nights. During this time the dog should sleep with or on the sock.

3 AFTER THE 48 HOURS are over, all the human subjects should place the socks in Ziploc bags and meet at your house.

4 ASK THE HUMAN subjects to wait in another room while you number the bags with a permanent marker or label. Make a note of which number bag goes with which dog. Close the bags.

5 ASK THE SUBJECTS to sniff the socks in all five bags and to name the one they think belongs to their dog.

WHAT TO EXPECT Some people may be better than others at identifying their dogs by smell.

WHAT'S GOING ON? Each individual dog has its smell, and owners may know them by it.

QUESTION THIS!

- Did your results surprise you?

- How could you test your results more widely?

- How could you do this experiment with human smells (that is, your family members)?

5

DOGS AND POINTING

Can you point out food to your dog?

CONCEPTS

DOMESTICATION, BEHAVIOR

HOW LONG IT TAKES
one day

WHAT YOU NEED
dog treats
two plates
a helper
two to five cups

Humans learn to point by about one year old. Other animals are less likely to respond to pointing. Some captive elephants can, and occasionally cats. But dogs are the champs. They watch humans intently—and have become experts at interpreting our body language. Of course, some dogs are better at this than others.

NOTE ABOUT DUMB DOGS
Dr. Brian Hare says that there are no dumb dogs, just dogs with different learning or behavioral styles. A dog that doesn't look to a person for directions may be better at solving problems for himself.

"Rosie is kind of a genius!"
—Nick

MAKE IT!

1 HAVE YOUR HELPER take your dog six to ten feet (1.8 to 3 m) away from you and have him sit facing you.

2 TAKE TWO TREATS and place them on plates at equal distances from your feet and either side of you, about 24 inches (61 cm) to your left and 24 inches (61 cm) to your right.

3 POINT TO ONE of the treats. Keep your finger pointed at it for the next two steps (4 and 5).

4 NOW SAY "OK." Call your dog and have your helper release him.

5 OBSERVE what happens.

6 LET YOUR DOG have both treats no matter which one he goes to first. (You are not training him, you are checking to see what he knows.)

> **WHAT TO EXPECT** Many dogs will go to the treat you pointed to first.

> **WHAT'S GOING ON?** Scientist Brian Hare says that dogs, like human children and some cats, understand and respond to pointing, realizing that it is designed to communicate information they need. Chimpanzees and wolves can't do this, so Hare thinks the ability is something that developed when dogs (and cats) were domesticated.

1-2

3

4

QUESTION THIS!

• Which remember where food is for a longer time, cats or dogs? How could you test this?

• Why do dogs and humans respond to pointing, but not chimps and wolves?

• Does this work with puppies or just adult dogs?

BONUS

a. With your dog in another room, hide a treat under one of two to five cups. When the dog comes in, point to the cup with the treat. How does your dog respond?

b. Let your dog watch you put the treat under a cup. Release her while pointing to the cup with the treat. How does your dog respond?

c. Let your dog watch you put the treat under a cup. Release her while pointing to a cup that doesn't have a treat. Which does your dog rely on more—her memory or your gesture?

CAT IQ TEST

Can your cat solve this problem?

CONCEPTS

BEHAVIOR, INTELLIGENCE, CAUSE AND EFFECT

HOW LONG IT TAKES
two hours, including assembly time (If you use more cats, factor in about twenty minutes per cat.)

WHAT YOU NEED
large box lid
screen mesh to fit the lid
craft tape or duct tape
scissors or a box cutter
two plastic spoons
string or plastic ties about 12 inches (30.5 cm) long
small cat treats or cat food
a cat or two or more

Here's one idea for checking a cat's IQ. Try this one—or make up your own puzzle for a cat to solve. A caution: A cat that doesn't pass your test may not be dumb. What else might be going on?

WHAT TO DO

1 MAKE THE TESTING apparatus.

a. Use the scissors or box cutter to cut a window out of the lid of the box. Cover the window with the mesh. This allows the cats to see in.

b. From one end of the box, cut a section out of the edge to allow the string and spoons to extend underneath.

2 TIE THE STRING or plastic ties to the spoon handles.

3 FILL THE SPOONS with cat food or treats and set them under the window so they are visible, with the ends of the strings or ties extending through the hole in the edge and beyond, on the floor.

4 BRING A CAT to the apparatus and let him explore. Observe the cat.

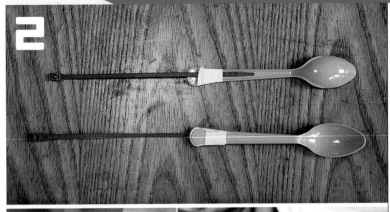

> **WHAT TO EXPECT** Some cats will make the connection between the treat they can see and the string or tie that is attached to it, and they will paw or pull at the tie to get the treat. But others may not figure it out at all—and certain cats will only figure it out some of the time.

> **WHAT'S GOING ON?** To solve this problem, the cat needs to be able to make the connection between the treat he can see, the string that is attached to the spoon holding the treat, and the end of the string that he can see outside the box. Then he needs to figure out that pulling the string will move the treat—and how to pull it so that he can get a hold of it.

> **FAIL!** It was hard to get cats to pay attention to this test. Taegu wouldn't come near the test at all. Olive checked it out, sniffing all around, but didn't try to interact with it. Jack pressed down on the screen and licked the food through it. Our conclusions: Maybe your cat has to be hungry when he takes this test in order to give results. Or maybe this test only looks at one way of solving the problem of getting the food—moving the ties and spoons.

"Jack isn't used to wet food, maybe that's why he tried to go through the screen to get it. But he's a good boy anyway."
—Jen

"See if he'll eat an ant."
—Mae

QUESTION THIS!

• Is this experiment a good indicator of cat intelligence? Why or why not?

• Is there another problem that might be a better indicator of how smart a cat is?

• Would this test be a good indicator of dog or human intelligence? Why or why not?

EGG TRICK #1

How do eggs react to acid?

CONCEPTS

REACTION OF CALCIUM CARBONATE
TO ACID

>>

HOW LONG IT TAKES
two days

WHAT YOU NEED
two eggs
pot for boiling eggs
water
stove
two glasses or jars to hold the eggs
vinegar
optional: food coloring

4-6

Shells—egg, clam, snail, or whatever—and bones are composed of calcium. They form to give structure and protection to animals. This experiment sheds light on what could happen in the ocean if the trend toward acidification continues. To find out more, Google *ocean acidification*.

WHAT TO DO

DAY ONE:

1 HARD-BOIL ONE EGG.
Place an egg in the pot and cover it with water. With adult assistance, boil it for three minutes, and let it stand for five minutes. Drain and cool.

> **GLITCH?** If boiling cracks your egg's shell, eat this one and boil another. You don't want any cracks in the shell for this experiment.

2 PLACE EACH EGG in a glass or jar. Label the glass to help you remember which egg is hard-boiled and which is raw.

3 POUR VINEGAR into the glasses to cover the eggs. If you want, add food coloring to the vinegar.

4 OBSERVE the eggs after an hour.

DAY TWO:

5 LET THE EGGS continue to soak in the vinegar for two days. Observe them again.

6 TAKE THE EGGS OUT of the vinegar and rinse them in cold water. What do you observe?

> **WHAT TO EXPECT** Bubbles should form on the outside of the eggs at first. Later the shells on the eggs should form a rubbery skin. One egg will be opaque, and the other will become translucent. One egg will have a stronger outer skin than the other. The size of the eggs may change as the eggshell becomes more eaten away and flexible.

> **WHAT'S GOING ON?** The calcium carbonate in the eggshell is a base. It reacts to the acetic acid in the vinegar by forming carbon dioxide (the bubbles). Here is the chemical reaction: $CaCO_3 + 2H^+ \rightarrow Ca^{+2} + H_2O + CO_2$

BONUS

RUBBER BONES

Clean an uncooked chicken bone and allow it to dry overnight. Test flexibility: bend but don't snap! Place in a jar of white vinegar. Each day for a week, remove the bone and test its flexibility. By the end of the week it should be bendy. This demonstrates how bone matrix (collagen—a protein found in bones—and minerals) is affected by acidic vinegar, which breaks down the minerals, leaving only collagen.

QUESTION THIS!

- Do the eggs move as they go through their reaction? How would you explain this?

- How can you explain the change in size?

DOUBLE BONUS:
EXOSKELETON VS. ENDOSKELETON

"Where's the rest of the shell? Ew, what happened to it?"
—Aaliyah

C ompare the effects of vinegar on other body parts, including exoskeleton and endoskeleton: fish bones, eggshells, crab claws, shrimp shells, snail shells, fingernail clippings, teeth . . .

OUR TRY

We used pairs of clam, mussel, crab, oyster, and snail shells from the beach. Most of the shells became soft and flexible, losing their brittleness and in some cases a brittle layer or two. The snail shell underwent the most dramatic change, so that at the end it looked like it had been naturally broken and worn away to start. But it had been shiny and intact just like the control that wasn't soaked in vinegar. In this photo, Aaliyah is looking at what's left of a blue mussel shell.

MAKE FOOTPRINT CASTS

Preserve a footprint to help with identification.

> **HOW LONG IT TAKES**
> an hour, not including the time it takes you to find a print

> **WHAT YOU NEED**
> casting material (plaster of paris or dental stone, one pound per casting)
> water
> three plastic containers, one containing plaster of paris, another containing water, and the third empty
> plastic measuring cup
> plastic spoon or chopstick for stirring
> sturdy shoebox or other container to carry home the cast
> tweezers
> hair spray or spray fixative (from art store)
> optional: a shoulder bag to carry your supplies, a camera

Remember when we left the cat carrier nearby (pages 38–39)? We also found big footprints in the mud nearby . . .

NOTE ABOUT CASTING

This project works great in sand and snow as well as soil. If you're casting in snow, cover the cast with plastic (a plastic bag will do) after pouring the plaster into the print, and leave it 40 to 45 minutes to solidify. With sand and snow, it's simple to just dig out around the cast, and take it along in a crusty pile. Once the plaster is completely firm, you can rinse it to get rid of the sand—and just let the snow melt.

MAKE FOOTPRINT CASTS
(CONTINUED)

WHAT TO DO

1 MAKE YOUR OWN footprint or find a print left behind by an animal.

2 TAKE A PHOTOGRAPH of the print. (This is optional, but it provides additional information.)

3 USE TWEEZERS to carefully remove leaves, bugs, stones, and other objects from the imprint. Then spray hair spray or fixative on the print.

4 MIX YOUR CASTING material as directed on its container. For instance, my plaster of paris required two parts of plaster to one part water (for example, two cups [.5 L] of plaster of paris and one cup of water [.25 L]). You want the casting material to have the consistency of a thick milkshake or cake batter.

5 POUR THE CASTING material into the imprint from one side, so that it fills the imprint gradually. Use the spoon to smooth it.

6 LET THE CAST SET for 20 minutes or more. The colder it is outside, the longer you should let the cast set.

7 REMOVE THE CAST by digging the entire impression out with your fingers. You're going to get dirty, but this is the only way to be sure you're picking up the cast in one piece. Place it in the shoebox.

8 LET THE CAST DRY overnight so that it is completely firm inside and out.

GLITCH?
• If your cast breaks in half or a chunk falls off while you're removing it from the print, don't freak out. You can glue it together once it's fully dry, using white glue. But if it crumbles completely, start over, and add a little more casting material to the water to make the cast more solid, or let it set a bit longer until it seems more solid.
• If there's dirt all over your cast, rinse it gently in cold water, and brush out the nooks and crannies with a soft paint brush.

WHAT TO EXPECT Your casting will help you to perceive details about the print that might not be visible otherwise.

WHAT'S GOING ON? The casting material sinks into the nooks and crannies of the impression and brings out details that you can use for animal identification.

OUR TRY
After the coyotes visited (see page 39), the dogs took a good sniff around the barn. The coyotes had been in a hurry, and they had been wrestling with the cat carrier and food, so we found only partial or messed-up footprints. But the sniffing dogs moved slowly and carefully, not sure what their noses were telling them, and leaving some good impressions in the mud. But whose pawprint was our cast? We matched the cast to our dogs' paws, and then to the culprit: neighbor dog Truffles!

5

7

8

BONUS:
REVERSE
PRINT

Once your cast is hard and dry, you can "walk" it into clay or wet sand to replicate the original footprint.

QUESTION THIS!

• What does an impression of a footprint show you that you wouldn't realize otherwise?

"Truffles, why didn't you scare away the coyotes?"

—me

65

NEARSIGHTED HOOPS

Are your hoops skills better with or without your glasses?

CONCEPTS

SCIENTIFIC PROCESS, CONTROLLING VARIABLES

HOW LONG IT TAKES
a day or two, or longer for more data

WHAT YOU NEED
a basketball hoop
chalk
your glasses
a notebook (or a partner with a notebook)

Vision issues can affect your depth perception, an important factor in the eye-hand coordination you need to shoot a basket. You may assume you're better with or without your glasses. Find out what the real story is, as Nikitha and Justin did.

WHAT TO DO

1 DETERMINE THREE positions from which you will shoot, and use chalk to mark them on your court or driveway with a number or letter.

2 TAKE THE SAME number of shots with and without your glasses from each position, and record the number of shots and baskets.

> **NOTE ABOUT THE SCIENTIFIC METHOD** Each time you test yourself, take shots in the same order, at the same time of the day. Record the weather conditions and how you feel, but try to keep every other variable consistent. That is, if you try jump shots from one position, try them from the others. Shoot the same way with and without your glasses.

3 ANALYZE YOUR DATA. Figure out your shot percentage (number of baskets divided by number of shots for each condition and position, multiplied by 100).

4 GRAPH YOUR DATA to create an easy visualization of your results.

> **WHAT TO EXPECT** Your results will vary depending on your vision and your ability to compensate for it.

"I'm definitely better with my glasses on."
—Justin

QUESTION THIS!

- How can you explain your results?

- Are you surprised by your results?

THINGS**WATER**DOES

t glows. It flows. It shows up in different forms in unexpected places. You can even use it to make friends—or enemies. (Be careful who you trick!)

HIGHLIGHTED WATER
PAGE 72

LIGHT-UP ICE BALL
PAGE 70

RAIN CLOUDS IN A BOTTLE
PAGE 75

WATER BEADS
PAGE 77

THE WET PENNY
PAGE 82

FLOATING WATER MAGIC TRICK
PAGE 79

LIGHT-UP ICE BALL

So pretty I've still got both of ours in the freezer.

CONCEPTS

WIRING AN **LED** TO A BATTERY, PROPERTIES OF ELECTRICITY, PROPERTIES OF WATER AND ICE

> ### HOW LONG IT TAKES
> two days

> ### WHAT YOU NEED
> medium-size balloon (We used round ones, but you can try other things.)
> LED
> electrical tape
> battery casing with wire leads attached
> AA battery
> bowl
> rubber band
> needlenose pliers
> paring knife or fingernail clipper

Water balloons + glowing lights + electronics + ice = a science experiment so cool and so inspiring we should charge admission!

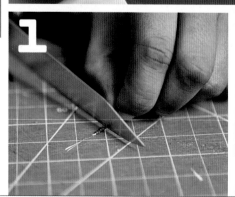

MAKE IT!

DAY ONE:

1 USE THE PARING KNIFE or fingernail clippers to remove ½ inch (1.3 cm) of insulation from the tips of the wire leads on the battery casing.

2 ATTACH THE POSITIVE (black) wire to the negative (shorter) end of the LED wire. Attach the negative (red) wire to the positive (longer) end of the LED wire.

3 TEST THE BATTERY. If it lights the LED, go ahead and wrap your connections in electrical tape.

4 INSERT THE LED in the balloon, leaving the battery casing outside.

5 FILL THE BALLOON with water, letting it expand like a water balloon. Use a rubber band to fasten the balloon's neck, leaving the battery and casing wired to the LED inside the balloon.

6 PLACE THE WATER balloon in a bowl and freeze it.

DAY TWO:

7 REMOVE THE ICE balloon from the freezer. Use a knife point to pierce the skin of the balloon, and peel the balloon off the ice.

WHAT TO EXPECT You should be able to see your LED's light shining through the ice that surrounds it. Isaac tested ours in a dark room.

WHAT'S GOING ON? Insulated wires, with connections protected with electrical tape, work fine with water surrounding them. The ice can obscure—or magnify and add sparkle to—the LED light.

QUESTION THIS!

• Which light is brighter—the LED by itself or the LED in ice?

• How would this project work with a balloon of a different shape?

HIGHLIGHTED WATER

Make your own Lake Eerie!

CONCEPTS

FLUORESCENCE, ULTRAVIOLET LIGHT

HOW LONG IT TAKES
one hour

WHAT YOU NEED

for blue:
tonic water, laundry detergent, or petroleum jelly

for other colors:
fluorescent-colored highlighter pens
water
knife
cutting board
rubber gloves
black or ultraviolet light or lightbulb

We can't quit coming up with variations on the theme of water that glows in the dark. How about the rainbow rose (page 10) with glowing water? What would that do to the colors in the rose? Or the ice ball (page 70), with glowing water—frozen, of course!—instead of plain? Here are some different ways to get that glow.

WHAT TO DO

1 MAKE BLUE: Tonic water glows very brightly when exposed to black or ultraviolet light. The quinine in the tonic water makes it glow bright blue under black light. We found that petroleum jelly (such as Vaseline) makes a dull blue glow, but certain laundry detergents glow brightly.

2 MAKE OTHER COLORS: Fluorescent dye can be extracted from a nontoxic highlighter pen, but some experimentation (and pen sacrifice) is needed. You'll need a sharp knife and a cutting board. Cut a highlighter pen in half (the short way). Pull out the ink-soaked felt/plastic-coated fibrous tube. Remove the tube with the ink and slice it open so that the ink can flow out of the fibers. You can soak the ink pad in water for a few hours or use gloved hands to squeeze the ink that is inside the pen into water. Soak the felt in a small amount of water.

WHAT TO EXPECT The liquid you create will glow in the dark when exposed to black light or ultraviolet light. You may need to experiment with different types and colors of highlighters before you find the ones that work the best.

Extra: Now you can add this dye to more water to make glowing fountains, grow certain kinds of glowing crystals, make glowing bubbles, or make glowing water beads.

WHAT'S GOING ON? Fluorescent compounds—such as quinine and chemicals in highlighters—absorb highly energetic but invisible ultraviolet light and release less energetic visible light. The water is transparent so it is easy to color with these glowing chemicals.

Note: You can store the glowing water in a sealed container and it will not go out or fade.

BONUS:
GLOWING HANDS

This isn't really an experiment, but it's so cool that it's irresistible. Use petroleum jelly (such as Vaseline) or laundry detergent on your hands. Put them up to a black light, and they should glow blue.

RAIN CLOUDS IN A BOTTLE

Done right, this one has the most rewarding whoosh.

CONCEPTS

WEATHER, CONDENSATION, PRESSURE

>> **HOW LONG IT TAKES**
about twenty minutes

>> **WHAT YOU NEED**
two-liter soda bottle, clean and dry (It's better with the labels removed, because you can see into the bottle clearly.)
rubbing alcohol
bicycle pump with needle
cork
skewer, drill bit, big needle, or something else you can use to make a path for the pump needle to go through the cork
optional: duct tape

For a better audience reaction to this action, work on your storytelling. How well can you explain the science behind the spectacle? (For hints, turn the page.)

RAIN CLOUDS IN A BOTTLE
(CONTINUED)

WHAT TO DO

1-2

1 FIT YOUR CORK to your bottle. You may need to shave the sides off the cork to get a tight fit. Your aim here is the tightest possible seal.

2 TRIM THE CORK to the length of the bike pump needle. You want the needle to be able to pass through the cork into the bottle, maintaining a tight seal.

5

3 MAKE A PATH for the cork, using your skewer, drill bit, or needle. Be sure the object you use to pierce the cork is narrower than the bike pump needle, or you won't have that tight seal I keep talking about.

4 WHEN THE CORK is ready, take it out of the bottle.

5 POUR ONE TEASPOON (5 mL) of rubbing alcohol into the bottle and screw the cap back on.

6 WITH THE CAP ON, turn the bottle horizontal and roll it so that the alcohol sloshes around and coats the inside of the bottle thoroughly and evenly.

7 INSERT the cork.

8 INSERT THE BIKE PUMP needle in the cork.

9 PUMP THE BIKE PUMP four or five times. Sometimes when you do this the cork will blow and you'll have your reaction. Other times you'll have to pump a few times more, then stop and pull the needle out.

8-9

6

7

WHAT TO EXPECT Once the pressure is released—either because the cork blows or the needle is removed—a cloud should form quickly and dramatically in the bottle.

Note: Aim the bottle away from you and anyone else. When Aaliyah pumped hard, our cork shot out and nearly hit Marco.

GLITCH? No cloud? Your seal isn't tight enough. Try a different cork, or use duct tape around the mouth of your bottle to tighten the seal.

WHAT'S HAPPENING? You're mimicking the part of Earth's water cycle in which evaporated water (water vapor) cools and condenses, forming clouds as they connect with dust. In this experiment, the alcohol acts like the dust, providing something cool for water droplets to attach to.

When you pressurize the soda bottle by pumping air in, the air molecules collide with each other and warm the bottle. Releasing the pressure causes the water vapor to condense quickly, forming a cloud.

BONUS

REVERSE THE EXPERIMENT!

Before the cloud disappears, put the needle back in and pump a couple more times. The cloud should disappear as quickly as it came. Release the pressure, and the cloud will reform.

NOTE ABOUT
WATER BEADS
They are sold under
lots of different
brand names,
including Water
Gems and Orbeez.

WATER BEADS

absorbing experience

NCEPTS

ERS / ABSORPTION / EVAPORATION

HOW LONG IT TAKES
one to three hours, including the
time it takes to make water
beads absorb water

WHAT YOU NEED
water beads
glass baking dish
water
food coloring
glow sticks

ater beads
are made of a
water-absorbing
polymer. They are sold
water source for plants. When seed water
s are placed in water, they can absorb more
100 times their weight in water, forming marble-
ed globes. Over time, they slowly release water back
heir surroundings. Water crystal gel, the absorbent material
osable diapers, is the powder form of water beads

WATER BEADS (CONTINUED)

1

2-3

5

4

1 MAKE WATER BEADS: Seed water beads look like tiny hard beads when you get them. But soak them in water for four to eight hours and they absorb the water, becoming jelly balls over time. They are fun to observe, time, and experiment with. Remove the water and watch them shrink, too. They'll shrink faster if laid on layers of absorbent paper towels.

2 SUBMERGE clear water beads in a dish of plain water. Ask a friend to identify what's in the dish. Then ask him to reach into it to prove if he's right. He'll encounter the water beads.

3 POUR THE WATER out of the dish, leaving the beads inside to show what the whole container of beads looks like.

4 SET THE DISH on top of a picture or flat sign. Ask your friend to try to identify the subject of the picture or read the words on the sign. He should have trouble, because the beads are in the way, distorting his view. Now pour water into the container. The beads will seem to disappear, and the sign or picture will become clear.

5 IN A DARK or dim room, submerge some glow sticks in the dish with the water beads. How does this affect their visibility?

BONUS

RAINBOW WATER BEADS

• The polymer in the beads will absorb the color in colored water. Pour blue and yellow water into a bowl of water beads, and see what color they come out.

• Color six or seven glasses of water in different colors and add water beads. They will absorb the colors, allowing you to use them to make patterns or layer them into rainbows.

"Ooh!"
—Cole

WHAT TO EXPECT The water beads are very hard to see when they are covered by water.

WHAT'S GOING ON? The water beds have almost the same refractive index as plain water, so when light comes through them it is not bent, making it almost impossible to see them.

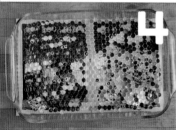

FLOATING WATER
MAGIC TRICK

You won't believe this can work.

My grandfather used to do these tricks in restaurants while we waited for our food. The longer we waited, the more tricks he did. How embarrassing!

It's true that there's no "magic" happening here, just real science. To add magical flair, work on your air of mystery and your interaction with your audience. Consider what to say and do to create the biggest "gee, whiz!" moment.

FLOATING WATER MAGIC TRICK (CONTINUED)

WHAT TO DO

1 PLACE THE PENNY in the glass of water.

2 HOLD THE CARD firmly over the mouth of the glass.

3 FLIP the glass.

> **WHAT TO EXPECT** If you do it right, holding the card very firmly, you'll only lose a little water when you flip the glass. Still, do it on a surface you can stand to get wet, and be prepared to practice a little to get the glass to retain the maximum amount of water.
>
> 1. Quickly slide the card out from under the glass.
> 2. Dry the area around the glass so that it looks like you had no spillage at all.

> **WHAT TO EXPECT THIS TIME** The water will shift down and rest right on the tabletop, held in place by the glass. The penny will appear under the water. But how to get it out? The only way is to slide the card back under again—or just lift the glass and get ready to mop up the mess.

> **WHAT'S GOING ON?** The water in the glass has enough pressure to "hold on" to the tabletop, just as it will hold onto the paper in the Double Bonus on page 81.

BONUS

DISAPPEARING GLASS MAGIC TRICK

This one requires vegetable oil and two glasses, one small enough to fit inside the other. Place the smaller glass inside the larger. Pour vegetable oil into the small glass. You'll be able to see the small glass. Do the next step while looking through the glasses from the side. Continue pouring as the vegetable oil overflows the smaller glass and fills the large one. The smaller glass should disappear from view.

DOUBLE BONUS: GLASS AND PAPER

Flip a glass of water over a sheet of paper just a little bigger than your glass. As you hold the glass upside down, the paper should stick over the mouth of the glass, and the water should stay inside.

"Why does that work?"
—Sossi

THE WET PENNY

Compare this trick with Egg Trick #2, page 86.

CONCEPTS

AIR PRESSURE, VACUUM, COMBUSTION, IGNITION

HOW LONG IT TAKES
twenty minutes, including setup

WHAT YOU NEED
a shallow bowl or dish
a tall water glass
a penny
a cork
matches
a thin knife, skewer, or needle

Here's another demonstration to help you put on a good show. Knowing what happens —the science "magic" behind the show—makes you the true master. Ask your audience what they think is happening before explaining the phenomenon.

OUR TRY

A full day after we finished this experiment, the glass still held the water firmly inside, and the dish and penny were still dry. We even moved it from one table to another without change. In the end, we took it apart to do the dishes, but we wondered how long it would last before some air made its way inside the glass and the water was released back into the dish.

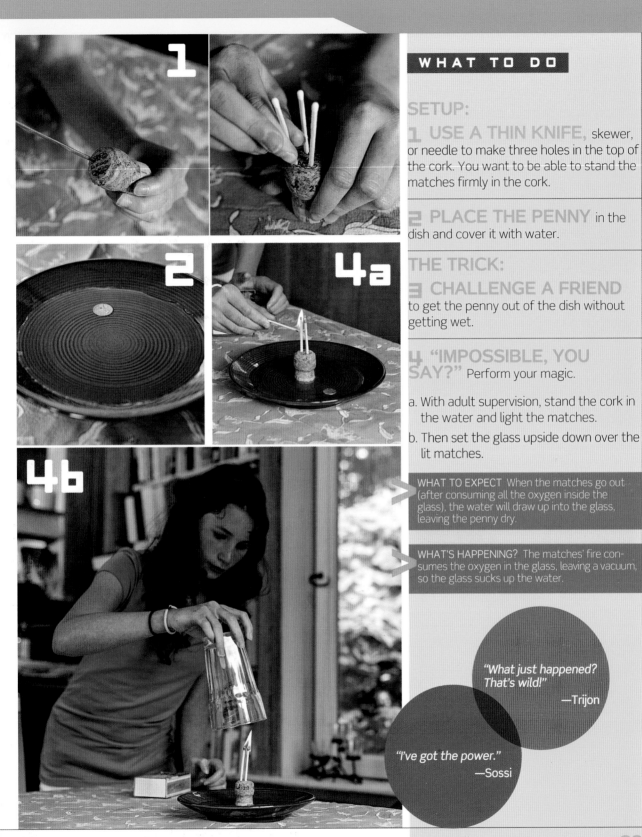

WHAT TO DO

SETUP:

1 USE A THIN KNIFE, skewer, or needle to make three holes in the top of the cork. You want to be able to stand the matches firmly in the cork.

2 PLACE THE PENNY in the dish and cover it with water.

THE TRICK:

3 CHALLENGE A FRIEND to get the penny out of the dish without getting wet.

4 "IMPOSSIBLE, YOU SAY?" Perform your magic.

a. With adult supervision, stand the cork in the water and light the matches.

b. Then set the glass upside down over the lit matches.

> **WHAT TO EXPECT** When the matches go out (after consuming all the oxygen inside the glass), the water will draw up into the glass, leaving the penny dry.

> **WHAT'S HAPPENING?** The matches' fire consumes the oxygen in the glass, leaving a vacuum, so the glass sucks up the water.

"What just happened? That's wild!"
—Trijon

"I've got the power."
—Sossi

REACTIONS

You know how scientists are often shown wearing lab coats? That's because sometimes science gets messy. These experiments are among our messiest, because the results can be somewhat unexpected. Get permission—and get things cleaned up afterward!

GHOST GLOVE
PAGE 88

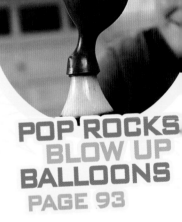

POP ROCKS BLOW UP BALLOONS
PAGE 93

EGG TRICK #2
PAGE 86

DANCING OOBLECK
PAGE 90

**COLORED
CANDY**
PAGE 96

**MYO
SUPER BALL**
PAGE 100

**WALKING ON
EGGS**
PAGE 98

**IVORY
SOAP FOAM**
PAGE 102

EGG TRICK #2

Can you make a jar inhale an egg?

CONCEPTS

COMBUSTION, IGNITION, VACUUMS

HOW LONG IT TAKES
thirty minutes

WHAT YOU NEED
hard-boiled egg (with saucepan, water, and a stove)
jar
matches

Compare this experiment with The Wet Penny (page 82). What physical phenomena do these two experiments let you demonstrate? Invent some new experiments: What else could be sucked into a vacuum you create?

NOTE ABOUT HARD-BOILED EGGS There was a controversy among us over how long it takes to hard-boil an egg. One faction put the egg in the water before heating it; that group boiled the egg for between three and five minutes. The other faction put the egg into water that was boiling; that group boiled the egg for ten or more minutes. Either way: same results? Decide for yourself. How does your family do it? Also, it seems like the only way to get the egg out is to break it apart with your fingers, but it's okay to eat it after this trick—unlike some of the other eggs-periments.

1

2b

2c

WHAT TO DO

1 PLACE A PEELED hard-boiled egg in the neck of a jar that is too small for the egg. (I found that a small jar that had held capers worked perfectly for my extra-large egg.)

2

a. Take the egg out of the jar neck.

b. With adult supervision, light two matches, and drop them into the jar.

c. Put the egg back on top.

3 YOUR EGG MAY drop all the way into the jar. (Note that ours did not!) If so, try blowing into the jar. What happens?

WHAT TO EXPECT When the matches go out, the egg will drop into the jar as if sucked in or inhaled. When you blow into the jar, the egg will pop back out again.

WHAT'S GOING ON? The lit matches eat up the oxygen in the jar, creating a drop of pressure (a vacuum) inside the jar. The pressure drop pulls the egg into the jar. When you blow into the jar, you raise the pressure in the jar above the pressure outside it, causing the egg to pop back out again.

QUESTION THIS!

• Why do you have to peel the egg?

• Would this reaction happen faster with three matches?

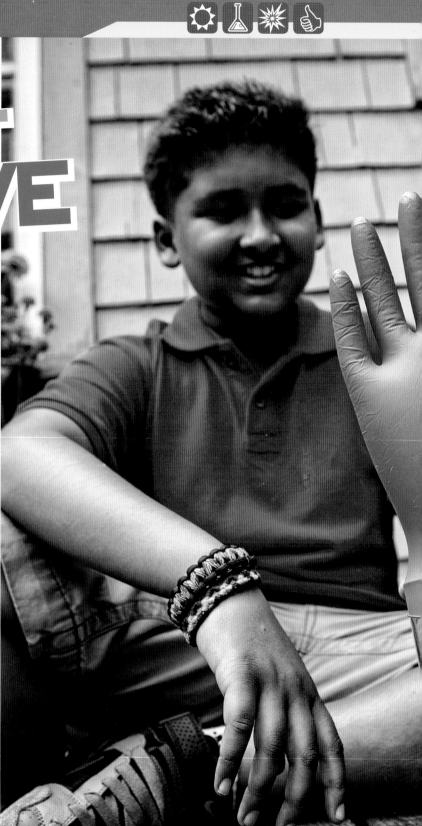

GHOST GLOVE

Making and splitting carbonic acid—and freaking out your friends.

CONCEPTS

CHEMICAL REACTIONS, ACIDS, BASES

HOW LONG IT TAKES
twenty minutes

WHAT YOU NEED
vinegar
baking soda
a glass
a surgical glove

This is a multistep reaction. Vinegar is acetic acid, and baking soda contains sodium bicarbonate, a base. They don't just mingle when mixed—their molecules rearrange into something else.

5

2

3

4

1 POUR THREE tablespoons (45 mL) of vinegar into the glass.

2 SPOON TWO teaspoons (10 mL) of baking soda into the glove. Hold the glove by the wrist and shake the baking soda down into the fingers.

3 HOLDING THE FINGERS of the glove shut, stretch the wrist of the glove over the mouth of the glass.

4 PULL THE GLOVE UP straight to let the baking soda fall into the vinegar.

5 OBSERVE what happens.

WHAT TO EXPECT As the baking soda reacts with the vinegar, it forms bubbles that inflate the glove.

WHAT'S GOING ON? When the sodium bicarbonate combines with the acetic acid, they form carbonic acid, which, in the second part of the reaction, divides into carbon dioxide and water. The carbon dioxide bubbles up, inflating the glove. At the end, what's left in the jar is sodium acetate.

Here's the chemical notation:

$$NaHCO_3(s) + CH_3COOH(l) \longrightarrow CO_2(g) +$$
baking soda   vinegar   carbon dioxide

$$H_2O(l) + Na+(aq) + CH_3COO-(aq)$$
water   sodium ion   acetate ion
       (sodium   (acetic acid)
       bicarbonate)

"That's epic!"
—Dylan

QUESTION THIS!

- Will this work with a balloon? How big a balloon?

DANCING OOBLECK

Out of the pages of Dr. Seuss …

CONCEPTS

NEWTONIAN PRINCIPLES, SOLIDS, LIQUIDS, GELS, SOUND WAVES, VIBRATION, RESONANCE

HOW LONG IT TAKES
one hour

WHAT YOU NEED
oobleck (cornstarch mixed with water)
food coloring
MP3 of audio test tone or other music
subwoofer (bass speaker) *See FAIL note, opposite!
plastic wrap
optional: metal pan and newspaper to add additional material to protect the speaker under the subwoofer, gloves

"It feels so weird. It's wet, but it feels dry."
—Abigail

What's oobleck? Oobleck is a non-Newtonian liquid, meaning it behaves unlike typical fluids. Flowing freely, it behaves as a regular liquid, but when a force is applied, it responds more like a solid. See also *Bartholomew and the Oobleck*, by Dr. Seuss.

top of the subwoofer. Or cover the sub-woofer with multiple layers of plastic wrap to protect it, and you can just plop the oobleck on top of the plastic to see it react to the sound. At first it will just lie there like a puddle . . .

NOTE: We used a stereo speaker plugged into a receiver and attached to the computer with a Y-cable that went into the headphone socket.

4 DOWNLOAD AN MP3
(sound file) of an audio test tone. One source: testsounds.com. You can also download a tone generator such as ToneGen, which allows you to test a range of sounds to see what works best.

5 SET UP the subwoofer to play a
test tone. Note: You can also just experi-ment with the bass of any music to see what it does to the oobleck. Experiment with the frequency of the subwoofer's bass until the oobleck begins to respond to it.

WHAT TO EXPECT The oobleck should form odd shapes and make movements in response to the vibrations of sound waves moving at dif-ferent frequencies and volumes.

GLITCH? If your oobleck does not respond, you may need to turn up the subwoofer or try a dif-ferent sound.

WHAT'S GOING ON? The pressure from the sound waves causes the oobleck to thicken as it moves.

FAIL! Our experiment went great, but we blew out our subwoofer because we left it playing one tone too long while we photographed the fabulous effect of this tone on the oobleck. There was a burning-rubber smell, and after that the speaker played without any bass tones. So change it up, keep down the volume, and keep your speaker healthy.

BONUS

WALKING ON OOBLECK

You can also make a huge batch of oobleck in a kiddie pool and try running on it.

QUESTION THIS!

• How will the oobleck respond to different sounds, different musical instruments, or different volumes?

WHAT TO DO

1 MAKE oobleck.

a. Combine one cup of water, 1½ to 2 cups (.35 to .5 L) of corn starch, and food color-ing to make oobleck. (It looks especially cool if you don't mix the food coloring in thoroughly, rather leaving it to form threads and bubbles of color.)

b. Mix it with your hands, adding corn starch until it stops sticking to your hands. Use gloves if you don't want food coloring to stain your hands.

2 PLAY WITH THE oobleck to
explore its unique properties.

3 YOU CAN TEST the oobleck's
response to sound in two ways. One way is to fill a metal pan with oobleck, set the speaker on its back, and place the pan on

BONUS:
DANCING SUGAR

Cover a jar with plastic wrap and secure with a rubber band. Sprinkle sugar on top. Nearby, bang a spoon on a cookie sheet. This demonstrates sonic boom and shows why the oobleck responds to the sounds in the previous activity.

POP ROCKS BLOW UP BALLOONS

Soda not fizzy enough? Try this!

CONCEPTS

GASES, MOLECULAR REACTIONS, NUCLEATION

HOW LONG IT TAKES
five minutes

WHAT YOU NEED
Pop Rocks candy
small balloons
bottle of soda
optional: surgical glove

When certain candy combines with soda, the results can be dramatic. For good reason, the experiments here are very popular on TV and the Internet—and there are various theories on what makes them work.

POP ROCKS BLOW UP BALLOONS (CONTINUED)

WHAT TO DO

1 POUR THE POP ROCKS into the uninflated balloon.

2 OPEN THE SODA bottle. Set the cap aside.

3 PINCH ABOVE the neck of the balloon to hold the Pop Rocks inside while stretching the neck of the balloon over the bottle neck.

4 RELEASE THE balloon, letting the Pop Rocks fall into the soda. Step back!

WHAT TO EXPECT The balloon should inflate. Janelle's didn't inflate as much as Jarrett's, but it did stand up straight.

WHAT'S GOING ON? Pop Rocks are made from pressurized carbon dioxide, which is a gas. When you place them in your mouth, the moisture reacts with the carbon dioxide, creating little pops. The bubbles in soda come from pumping carbon into the syrup (in a process called carbonation). So the soda also has pressurized carbon dioxide. When you add Pop Rocks to soda, the bubbles that result are big enough to inflate the balloon.

NOTE: You can also try this with a surgical glove, which will be thinner than a typical balloon, for comparison. See Ghost Glove, page 88.

QUESTION THIS!

• What's the smallest number of Pop Rocks that will inflate the balloon?

• Will different kinds of soda have different reactions? How about diet vs. regular?

• How could you increase the amount of inflation you get from this reaction?

BONUS: SODA BOTTLE ROCKET

Diet Coke + Mentos candy + index cards to control the situation = fountain gush!

> **WHAT YOU NEED**
two-liter bottle of Diet Coke
a package of Mentos mint candy
two index cards
transparent tape

"I got wet!"
—Caitlyn

"That went like two stories high!"
—Janelle

WHAT TO DO

1 USE ONE INDEX CARD to roll a tube slightly larger than the width of the Mentos, and fasten this tube with tape.

2 NOW TAKE THE CAP off the soda and cover the bottle opening with the other index card, laid flat.

3 STAND THE INDEX CARD tube atop the bottle opening, and fill it with the Mentos.

4 SLIDE OUT the flat index card and step away.

WHAT TO EXPECT As the Mentos fall into the soda, they'll react with the soda and create a gushing fountain that can shoot 20 to 30 feet (6 to 9 m) high.

WHAT'S GOING ON? When people first discovered this reaction, they thought it had to do with the sweeteners, acid, or caffeine combining. But scientists, who are still working on this problem, now think that the reaction isn't chemical, but physical. The carbon dioxide molecules in the soda merge to form bubbles on the surface of the Mentos candy. It happens especially well with this candy because its surface is as pitted as a golf ball. This non-shiny, non-flat surface allows nucleation, meaning that the pits make for easy bubble-forming. As these bubbles escape to the surface, they push the soda in front of them, creating the gusher.

QUESTION THIS!

• How will other candy respond to soda?

COLORED CANDY

Candy-coating, revealed

CONCEPTS

SOLUTIONS, SUSPENSIONS, COLORS, PIGMENTS

> **HOW LONG IT TAKES**
> two to three hours

> **WHAT YOU NEED**
> petri dishes
> water
> clock or timer
> colored candies

I like candy. Who doesn't? Who wouldn't like something that is designed for enjoyment, not just tasty, but sweet to the eyes as well. How do they do that? This experiment helps you get to the bottom of the mystery of colorful candy-coating—including the mystery of one favorite candy whose color actually changes as you suck on it.

WHAT TO DO

1 FILL EACH PETRI DISH with water and put a colored candy in.

2 WATCH THE COLORS dissolve at different rates.

3 YOU CAN ALSO experiment with other liquids to see how the colors behave in different solutions, or in liquids at different temperatures.

WHAT TO EXPECT The colors will change at different rates depending on the color, the liquid, and the temperature of the solution.

WHAT'S GOING ON? The solid candy melts into the water or other liquid to create a solution that has its own color. Different pigments (solids used to create colors) dissolve (enter solutions) at different rates.

QUESTION THIS!

• Does it make a difference if the colored candy has a flavor or not?

• Do different candies with the same color dissolve at the same rate?

• What happens to candies that have writing or other symbols stamped onto them?

• What will happen if you place two or more candies of different colors in the same dish? Can you make new colors this way?

"I wonder if Coke or seltzer—something carbonated—would melt the coating of the candy faster?"

—Brandon

OUR TRY

Gobstoppers are particularly great with this because they have layers of colors. We also tried Skittles and M&Ms.

BONUS

EXPANDING GUMMIES

Place a gummy bear or other gummy in a petri dish full of water overnight. What happens to it by morning?

WALKING ON EGGS

Distribute your weight evenly … then wait.

CONCEPTS

WEIGHT DISTRIBUTION AND DYNAMICS, PACKAGING, CUSHIONING

HOW LONG IT TAKES
one hour

WHAT YOU NEED
at least four one-dozen cartons of eggs (the cartons preferably made of varied materials: cardboard, plastic, Styrofoam)
a curb or low stool
your bare feet
optional: crutches, a cane, a railing, a staircase with a bannister

Do you feel like you're walking on eggshells around us? You could be. Eggshells are specially made to protect what's inside—and so are egg cartons. See how much pressure they can take.

1

"Cracks are forming!"
—Dylan

WHAT TO DO

1 HERE'S THE IDEAL setup; try to replicate it or to create a similar situation.

A porch stoop with a railing on each side. Place the open egg carton on the sidewalk and stand on the lowest step. Holding the railings, gently place your bare feet atop the eggs. Carefully shift your weight until you are standing squarely on top of the eggs, then let go of the railings.

2 REPEAT WITH the other two boxes of eggs, being careful to do it the same way each time.

> **WHAT TO EXPECT** You are highly likely to break or crack some eggs, but one package type may triumph over the others in terms of cushioning effect.

> **WHAT'S HAPPENING?** Different materials respond in various degrees to the weight of your body atop the eggs.

QUESTION THIS!

• What would happen if you closed the cover of the egg carton before standing on it?

• How well would the box cushion the eggs if you just jumped on them or stood on them without taking the trouble to distribute your weight evenly?

• Does it make a difference whether the smaller ends of the eggs are turned up or down?

• How would you design an egg box that would do a better job of cushioning the eggs?

MYO SUPER BALL

Ready to bounce?

CONCEPTS

POLYMERS, CHEMICAL REACTION, RATIOS

HOW LONG IT TAKES
thirty minutes

WHAT YOU NEED
borax (found in the laundry section of the grocery store)
cornstarch (found in the baking section of the store)
white glue such as Elmer's (makes an opaque ball) or blue or clear school glue (makes a translucent ball)
warm water
food coloring
spoon
small containers for mixing
measuring spoons

What makes something bounce? Here's a recipe for finding the bounce in a combination of ingredients. Try different amounts of the materials and different combinations of mixing and kneading times until you hit upon the best formula.

QUESTION THIS!

• How will changing the procedure and proportions (ratio between the amounts of glue, cornstarch, and borax) change the outcome?

• How could you make a more stretchable ball? A gooier ball? A slimier ball? A bigger ball?

NOTE ABOUT FOOD COLOR
If you want to add color, you can add some food coloring to your mixture while stirring.

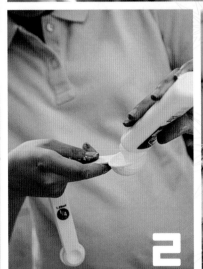

1 MAKE BORAX solution. Combine two tablespoons (30 mL) of warm water and ½ teaspoon (2.5 mL) of borax powder. Stir to dissolve the borax. Add food coloring, if desired. You'll have enough to make seven or eight balls.

FOR EACH BALL:

2 USE A DIFFERENT bowl. Pour in one tablespoon (15 mL) of glue. Add ½ teaspoon (2.5 mL) of the borax solution and one tablespoon of cornstarch. Do not stir. Allow the ingredients to interact on their own for ten to fifteen seconds.

3 THEN STIR THEM together to fully mix. Once the mixture becomes impossible to stir, take it out of the cup and start molding the ball with your hands. The ball will start out sticky and messy, but it will solidify as you knead it.

4 ONCE THE BALL is less sticky, go ahead and bounce it.

> **WHAT TO EXPECT** Your ball will solidify and become bounceable.

> **WHAT'S GOING ON?** Polymers are molecules made up of repeating chemical units. (By the way, a single one of those units is called a monomer.) Glue contains the polymer polyvinyl acetate (PVA), which cross-links to itself when it reacts to being combined with borax.

"Which color bounces highest? Does it make a difference?"
—Marco

IVORY SOAP FOAM

What makes it do that?

CONCEPTS
PHYSICAL AND CHEMICAL CHANGES, HEAT

HOW LONG IT TAKES
five minutes

WHAT YOU NEED
Ivory soap
large microwavable bowl
microwave oven

What's foam? Foam is the substance that forms when pockets of gas are trapped inside a solid or liquid "matrix" material. Examples include cream, egg whites, sea water, and even soap. As the matrix material ferments or is shaken or agitated by heating, bubbles form and combine, expanding the matrix into foam.

1

WHAT TO DO

1 PLACE A BAR OF IVORY soap in the microwavable bowl and microwave it for 90 seconds.

2 REMOVE THE BOWL from the microwave and play with the foam.

WHAT TO EXPECT The soap will turn into foam—aerated, softened soap.

WHAT'S GOING ON? Ivory soap has more air inside than other soaps, making it a good matrix material. (Note that this is also what makes it float, a famous advertising point.) When the air and water inside the soap are heated, they expand, creating a physical change, rather than a chemical change. The result is a fluffy cream, similar to whipped cream—but soapy!

"It looks like it's breathing."
—Serenity

"It feels like ice cream."
—Adriana

QUESTION THIS!

• What happens to other soaps when you microwave them?

• What happens to the Ivory soap foam over time?

WEIRDPHYSICS

Isn't life strange? Maybe you don't think so now, but you'll KNOW so after trying the activities in this chapter. Open your mouth and say "Awe!"

BIKE WHEEL
GYROSCOPE
PART 1
PAGE 108

MYO GIANT
AIR CANNON
PAGE 106

BIKE WHEEL
GYROSCOPE
PART 2
PAGE 110

SWIMMING WITH CLOTHES ON
PAGE 112

DIET COKE VS. COKE FLOATING SMACKDOWN
PAGE 118

ICE-SKATER EFFECT
PAGE 120

FROZEN BOUNCE
PAGE 115

MYO GIANT AIR CANNON

Have a blast (of air)!

CONCEPTS

FLUID DYNAMICS, BERNOULLI'S PRINCIPLE, CONSERVATION OF ENERGY

HOW LONG IT TAKES
one hour

WHAT YOU NEED
20- or 30-gallon (77- or 98-L) plastic trash can
clear plastic shower curtain
bungee cord
scissors or craft knife
optional: paper cups, colored smoke balls (also called smoke bombs)

Bernoulli's principle applies to:

- putting "spin" on a table-tennis ball or a tennis ball (using uneven pressure to do it)
- "bending" a soccer ball with that same spin, as David Beckham famously did
- spraying a water hose by pinching it
- this air cannon

"That is majestically glorious."
—Stephanie

QUESTION THIS!

- What's the maximum distance at which your air cannon will work to knock down the cup or blow back someone's hair?

WHAT TO DO

1 WITH ADULT supervision, use the craft knife to cut a circle six to eight inches (15 to 20 cm) in diameter in the bottom center of the trash can. Note: Often these cans have a circle in the center. Just cut out that circle.

2 STRETCH THE SHOWER curtain material across the open top end of the trash can and fasten it with a bungee cord. Use scissors to trim the excess shower curtain, leaving three or four inches (8 to 10 cm) hanging below the bungee cord.

3 TO WORK THE AIR cannon, lift the trash can by one handle and hold it horizontally over your shoulder or against your hip. Give the shower curtain membrane a sharp pat in the center.

> **WHAT TO EXPECT** When you pat the shower curtain, a puff of air should come out of the opening at the bottom end. You can set up the cups as a target and practice shooting the air at them to knock them over. Or see if a friend notices the puff of air hitting him.

> **WHAT'S GOING ON?** Bernoulli's principle explains what happens when you pinch a garden hose to make water squirt out. When you narrow the hose, you create a vortex, which makes the fluid at the center of the flow move faster than the fluid along the edges. So the water's velocity increases as its pressure decreases. In the air cannon, the same principle applies to air that is pushed unevenly through the hole in the trash can.

"Quit shooting air at me!"
—Patsy

BONUS

SMOKE RINGS

You can blow smoke rings with your air cannon, using colored smoke from a smoke bomb. Do this outside! Have an adult set the smoke bomb and light it. Place the hole of your air cannon over the smoke bomb, and let the air cannon sit until it fills with colored smoke. Lift the cannon and pat the membrane to blow a smoke ring.

BIKE WHEEL GYROSCOPE
PART 1

How does a bicycle stay up?

CONCEPTS

ANGULAR MOMENTUM, PRECESSION, GYROSCOPE

HOW LONG IT TAKES

thirty minutes (including assembly time)

WHAT YOU NEED

a BMX bicycle wheel or other small solid-axle wheel with pegs attached
clothesline (strong enough to support the weight of the wheel)
bicycle handles to extend the wheel's axis
doorway or overhang with a nail or hook to hold the clothesline

This experiment helps you see how a bicycle works. If you've ever tried to see how slowly you can pedal before you lose your balance, you've already experimented with the principles explored here.

WHAT TO DO

1 ATTACH THE BICYCLE

pegs to each side of the wheel's axis. This gives you a way to hold the wheel so that it can spin freely.

2 TIE THE CLOTHESLINE

firmly to one side of the axle, between the peg and the wheel.

3 SUSPEND THE BICYCLE

wheel by the cord from an overhang or doorway. We used a nail in the beam at the top of the porch. You can tie it, but we had a friend hold the end of the clothesline to just keep it hung firmly over the nail.

4 SPIN THE WHEEL as fast as you can.

GLITCH? Wheel won't spin? If your line is too thick, it can impede the spinning. Try thinner clothesline.

WHAT TO EXPECT When spinning, the wheel should hang not exactly vertically, but at about 75 to 80 degrees from horizontal. It should also circle the line in one direction or the other. As it slows, it will spin in a helix pattern before flattening out to horizontal again.

WHAT'S GOING ON? This experiment demonstrates two principles: precession (a spinning object orbits its axis) and angular momentum (a circular-moving force that happens because the mass of the wheel is mainly in its rim). A bicycle gains stability as it goes faster—because it maintains the angular momentum of the wheels.

QUESTION THIS!

- Why is it hard to ride a bike extremely slowly?

- What's the relationship between this experiment and a "sleeping" yo-yo?

"So that's why a bike keels over when you slow down . . ."
—Nick

BIKE WHEEL GYROSCOPE
PART 2

Feel the force!

ANGULAR MOMENTUM, INERTIA, VELOCITY,
FRICTION, TORQUE

HOW LONG IT TAKES
fifteen minutes

WHAT YOU NEED
a BMX bicycle wheel or other small
solid-axle bike wheel with pegs
attached, as in the first Bike Wheel
Gyroscope experiment, page 108
a swivel chair
a partner

You're used to the idea that pushing the pedals on a bike powers the bike. Here's what happens when a bicycle wheel is used to power you as you sit on a swivel chair instead of the seat of the bike. For comparison, sit on a chair that doesn't swivel.

WHAT TO DO

1 SIT IN A SWIVEL chair.

2 HOLD THE WHEEL by its pegs. Place the wheel in a vertical position.

3 HAVE YOUR PARTNER set the wheel spinning.

4 TURN THE WHEEL so that it spins horizontally. What happens?

5 NOW TURN the still-spinning wheel over so that it's spinning in the opposite direction. What happens?

6 NOW HOLD the spinning wheel vertically. What happens?

WHAT'S GOING ON? Torque is a principle of a spinning object, a force that keeps it turning in a horizontal plane. This is what turns you as the angular momentum of the wheel is maintained by the spin. (This is the odd force you feel as the wheel causes your whole body to turn in the chair.) When you turn the wheel over, the force reverses direction. But holding the wheel vertically will not turn the chair.

"You can feel a force pulling at you."
—Adriana

QUESTION THIS!

How does it feel to hold the spinning wheel horizontally when you're not in a swivel chair?

SWIMMING WITH CLOTHES ON

It's kind of a drag.

CONCEPTS

DRAG, FLUID DYNAMICS, AERODYNAMICS

> **HOW LONG IT TAKES**
> an hour or two

> **WHAT YOU NEED**
> a swimming pool
> a swimsuit
> street clothes
> a stopwatch
> a notebook
> a pair of pants
> a partner and adult supervision

Lifesavers practice swimming in their clothes in order to be prepared for how that feels. They need to know how to adapt their swim to deal with the additional drag created by wet fabric. Go beyond "how it feels" by measuring the difference clothes and swimsuits make to the speed of your swim.

NOTE OF CAUTION
Never swim alone.

WHAT TO DO

1 HAVE YOUR PARTNER time your laps.

2 SWIM TEN LAPS, alternating what you're wearing each time. The first lap, swim in your swimsuit.

3 THE SECOND LAP, put on clothes. Decide what clothes you'll wear. You can assess the effects of wearing shoes, jeans, and a sweatshirt, or lighten up a little with shorts and a t-shirt.

4 COMPARE YOUR swimming times with and without clothes.

NOTE You'll get tired—and possibly slow down—as you swim your laps. The purpose of alternating is to try to keep your energy level equal.

WHAT TO EXPECT Your first lap, in the swimsuit, will probably be fastest. Your last lap, in clothes, slowest of all.

WHAT'S HAPPENING? As your clothes fill with water, they will weigh you down. This is increased drag. When you wear your swimsuit, you help make your body more streamlined and aerodynamic, decreasing drag.

"That's 23 seconds with clothes on and 13 seconds with a swimsuit on."
—Doug

QUESTION THIS!

• Which fabrics create the most drag?

• What strokes are easier or harder when you're wearing clothes while swimming?

BONUS:
MAKE YOUR OWN LIFE JACKET

What would you do to stay afloat if you somehow fell in the water wearing clothes? Lifesavers learn to take off jeans or other pants in the water, to tie the ankles together in a big overhand knot, zip the jeans, and "inflate them" by filling them with water. Try this, then put the ankle knot behind your head and put your head through the legs to create a life vest. Why do you think filling the jeans with water allows them to float?

NOTE OF CAUTION
This is not an approved floating device.
(But it sure could help in an emergency!)

FROZEN BOUNCE

Does temperature affect bounce?

CONCEPTS

ELASTICITY, TEMPERATURE, BOUNCE

>> **HOW LONG IT TAKES**
three hours (including freezing time)

>> **WHAT YOU NEED**
two tennis balls
a freezer
a wall, basketball hoop pole, or stepladder to drop ball from (we used a ladder)
chalk or string (we used "flag" tape ties, just because they were handy) for measuring the wall, pole, or stepladder
a metal tape measure

I f you tried MYO Super Ball (page 100), you're aware that materials make a difference when it comes to how much a ball will bounce. In this experiment, you'll look at other conditions that could affect bounce. Once you've analyzed the conditions here, create some new ball drops: wet vs. dry; inflated vs. not so full—whatever you can think of!

WEIRDPHYSICS

WHAT TO DO

1 PLACE A TENNIS ball in the freezer for at least two hours.

2 USE YOUR TAPE measure and chalk to mark out measurements on the wall, pole, or ladder. You can do this as you bounce the ball, using a different color chalk for each ball, or draw measurement markings on the wall ahead of time and record each ball's bounces in a notebook.

3 BOUNCE THE unfrozen tennis ball and see how high it bounces. In doing this, establish how you will bounce the ball, from what height, so that you can replicate the technique with the frozen ball. Bounce the unfrozen tennis ball at least ten times and record the measurements.

4 REPEAT with the frozen tennis ball.

WHAT TO EXPECT One of the balls will bounce higher than the other.

WHAT'S HAPPENING? When a material is frozen, its molecules contract, becoming more dense and causing it to become less flexible.

QUESTION THIS!

• How would your results change if you froze the tennis ball for longer?

• What difference does the surface on which you're bouncing the ball make?

• What difference does the height from which you bounce the ball make?

• What difference does the force with which you bounce the ball make?

BONUS:
BASKETBALL
BALL BOOST

Place a tennis ball on top of a basketball and let them both drop. What happens?

WHAT TO EXPECT The tennis ball will bounce surprisingly high.

WHAT'S HAPPENING? The basketball is heavier and lower, so it hits the ground first and bounces back up, hitting the tennis ball and transferring its momentum to the smaller ball, so the tennis ball goes higher than it would on its own.

"Whoa!"
—Brandon

DIET COKE vs. COKE
FLOATING SMACKDOWN

Which one floats?

CONCEPTS
CONCEPTS

BUOYANCY, DENSITY

HOW LONG IT TAKES
five minutes

WHAT YOU NEED
two cans of the same kind of soda, one diet and one regular
a container of water, such as an aquarium, a bathtub, a large pot or bucket

W ill it float? A popular TV show asked this question, before dropping all sorts of items into containers of water. The audience and celebrities made predictions—and the outcomes were frequently surprising. Try that—and try this! When it comes to buoyancy, it can be tricky to hypothesize about what will and won't float.

1

BONUS:
RAINBOW
IN A JAR

Use light corn syrup, olive oil, Dawn dishwashing liquid, rubbing alcohol, and water. Determine which is most dense (and will sink to the bottom), which is least dense (and will rise to the top), and how the layers between will organize themselves, according to their density. Then use food coloring to color them each according to their density in order to create a rainbow. Finally, pour equal amounts of each liquid into the jar to test your density prediction.

WHAT TO DO

PLACE BOTH CANS of soda in the water. Observe what happens.

WHAT TO EXPECT One can should float and one should sink.

WHAT'S GOING ON? The regular soda has about ten teaspoons (50 mL) of sugar, with a density greater than that of water—more matter packed into a smaller space. But the diet soda has artificial sweetener, which is sweeter than sugar, so that less is required to make the sweet taste. The diet soda is less dense, so it floats.

QUESTION THIS!

• Does this work with other flavors of soda?

• What about other kinds of drinks with artificial sweeteners, such as iced tea?

119

ICE-SKATER EFFECT

Try a skater's spin—without ice.

CONCEPTS

INERTIA, ANGULAR MOMENTUM, FRICTION, VELOCITY

HOW LONG IT TAKES
fifteen minutes (including assembly time)

WHAT YOU NEED
two two-pound (.9-kg) hand weights
a swivel chair

Have you seen an ice-skater spin, bringing her hands in and out to increase her motion? This is what you're doing—without ice skates! As you bring your hands and arms (and weights) closer to your body, you move mass closer to the vertical axis of your rotation. You can use this information to speed up or slow your spin.

WHAT TO DO

1 SIT in the swivel chair.

2 HOLD THE WEIGHTS IN your hands and start to turn.

3 HOLD THE WEIGHTS AT chest level and open your arms to the side, with your elbows slightly bent. Now bend your elbows more and pull the weights in to your chest together. Continue this motion—in and out with the weights—to see how it affects your spin.

> **GLITCH?** The weights and your arm action don't get you moving? Start yourself with your feet, and then start the motion.

> **NOTE ABOUT SPINNING** Spotting is something dancers learn to do when they spin to keep from getting dizzy and to stay in control. Pick a spot on the wall, and as you spin, look for that spot, turning your head quickly to get to it.

> **WHAT TO EXPECT** The tighter, smaller motion (with the elbows bent all the way as you bring the weights to your chest) should increase your spin.

> **WHAT'S GOING ON?** In a spin, you reach a balance between inertia (no motion) and friction (in which motion slows). You spin faster when you pull your hands and the weights in, because you pull mass toward the center of the spin (its vertical axis).

QUESTION THIS!

- What part of the motion slows you down the most?
- How long can you keep spinning using the weights?
- Does the weight of the weights make a difference?
- Does the weight of the person doing the experiment change the outcome?

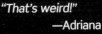

"That's weird!"
—Adriana

MACHINES

Try this, and that, and the other—until you make these machines work. Do it our way or your way. If you hit a glitch or a fail, don't despair. You're not the only one! If at first you don't succeed, try, try again.

HOVER BALLOON
PAGE 126

MECHANICAL DISSECTION
PAGE 124

RACING ROCKET BALLOONS
PAGE 127

MAKE A SUNDIAL
PAGE 130

MINI-SPINNERS
PAGE 135

BRUSHYBOTS
PAGE 132

HUMAN SLINGSHOT
PAGE 137

MECHANICAL DISSECTION

Take something apart, and put it back together again. Does it still work?

CONCEPTS

MACHINES, PROCESSES, FORM, FUNCTION, ENGINEERING AND REVERSE ENGINEERING, MECHANICS, DESIGN

HOW LONG IT TAKES

an hour or two, or a year or two, depending on the object you take apart

WHAT YOU NEED

a wind-up toy or other mechanical toy, or a household object that is a machine with multiple parts, such a doorknob. (You can also do this with an old appliance or a car.)
an undisturbed work space
You'll figure out what tools you need as you work, for example, a wrench or screwdriver
optional: notebook, sketchbook, laptop computer, camera

G o slowly as you take apart a machine. You'll learn new skills, and get an understanding of how it works. You'll gain confidence to put it back together, then take apart something more complex.

OUR TRY

Brandon took apart a bike and Niyanna took apart a desktop pencil sharpener. Niyanna put the desktop pencil sharpener back together, but we gave the bike away for parts.

1

NOTE OF WARNING
It's not a good idea to take apart certain electronics, particularly printers.

1 BEGIN SLOWLY to take apart your machine. As you do, take pictures and notes as a record of what you do. Or develop your own system for recalling what goes where and how each part relates to others, a "build list" that guides you as you put the machine back together again.

2 TO TEST YOURSELF part way through, put a few parts back on the machine. Then take them off again and keep going. This way you'll build confidence that you can put the machine back together at the end.

3 WHEN THE MACHINE is fully disassembled, put it back together.

4 TEST THE FUNCTION of the machine to make sure you have put it together properly. If it doesn't work, or works differently than before, try again.

> **WHAT TO EXPECT** Engineers throughout history have learned their craft by taking apart machines, with different results. Not being able to get something back together correctly is a normal part of this process, so be sure not to take apart a machine that you can't live without or would be truly sorry to wreck.

> **WHAT'S GOING ON?** You're observing how a machine is made and how the parts fit together to create the functions you see when the machine is working.

QUESTION THIS!

- What went right?
- What went wrong?
- What did you learn about this machine that surprised you?
- What questions do you have about this machine?
- What did you learn about yourself by doing this?
- What advice would you give to someone else who tried this?
- How would you do things differently next time?

HOVER BALLOON

Ready for liftoff?

CONCEPTS

AERODYNAMICS, JET PROPULSION, AIR PRESSURE, HYDROFOILS

> **HOW LONG IT TAKES**
> thirty minutes to an hour

WHAT YOU NEED
CD
balloon
soda bottle cap
drill
hot glue gun and glue sticks
tabletop or smooth floor

What's a hovercraft? It's a vehicle that blows an air cushion under itself to produce lift. As the vehicle is propelled forward, it floats above the surface—land, sea, or your tabletop.

QUESTION THIS!

• How could you improve the way these hover balloons work?

WHAT TO DO

1 DRILL a hole in the center of a soda bottle cap.

2 HOT-GLUE the bottle cap to the CD, centering it over the hole in the center of the CD.

3 BLOW UP THE BALLOON and, while pinching the neck closed, stretch the neck of the balloon over the bottle cap.

4 SET THE CD on the table or floor and release the balloon.

WHAT TO EXPECT The hover balloon will scoot around the tabletop.

WHAT'S GOING ON? The air inside the balloon releases down out of the balloon and creates a cushion of air under the CD, which moves around because the air cushion is uneven.

GLITCH? This is a little tricky, but we got the hang of it and you will, too. It's easier if you stretch the neck of the balloon before trying to fit it over the bottle cap. You can also have a friend fit the balloon on the bottle cap for you while you hold the balloon closed.

RACING ROCKET BALLOONS

Fun that goes *pffffft*

CONCEPTS

JET PROPULSION, AERODYNAMICS, MECHANICS, FRICTION

HOW LONG IT TAKES

one hour

WHAT YOU NEED

wire or string
balloons
hockey tape, electrical tape, or another cloth tape
plastic straws
optional: permanent markers

This is fun to do with a few other people, so you can race your balloons.

RACING ROCKET
BALLOONS
(CONTINUED)

1 INFLATE A BALLOON. If you want, draw a face or wings or messages on your balloon.

2 USE TWO PIECES of tape to attach a straw to it. Attach the straw so that its ends are toward the top and bottom of the balloon. Now let the balloon deflate.

TO SET UP THE RACE COURSE:

3 MEASURE THE distance you want your balloon to travel. For example, if you want it to rocket across the room, measure the room. Then cut a piece of wire or string that length. Attach one end of it to the wall at the other end of the room or to a piece of furniture.

4 THREAD THE LOOSE end of the wire through the straw on your balloon, starting at the top and ending at the bottom.

5 ATTACH THE END of the wire to a railing or chair back in front of you. (See picture 6.)

6 ALL TOGETHER, blow up your balloons and pinch the neck to hold the air in.

7 READY, SET, LET GO! At the signal, let go of your balloon and let it fly along the wire.

WHAT TO EXPECT Your balloon may—or may not—zip along the wire or string. It depends on the angle and length of the "race course" and the positioning and length of the straw.

WHAT'S GOING ON? As the air shoots out of the balloon, it propels the balloon along the wire or string.

GLITCH? Balloons don't go? Consider changing the position of the straw, or using a longer or shorter piece of straw.

QUESTION THIS!

- What difference do the angle and length of the wire make?

- What shape balloon works best?

- What amount of air works best?

- What works best: small or large balloons? Oblong or long ones?

- What works best: wire or string?

BONUS:
SKEWER YOUR BALLOON

Try poking a skewer (metal or bamboo like ours) through a balloon. Blow up a balloon and knot it. Insert the point of the skewer next to the knot, through the balloon, and out the other end where there's a dark spot on the balloon's skin. (With thanks to Jarrett Nunes for the tip.)

"The skewer can go through the balloon because the polymer (balloon material) wraps around the skewer, which makes the air not leak out."
—Jarrett

MAKE A SUNDIAL

Map the time of your life.

CONCEPTS

ASTRONOMY, MOVEMENT OF THE SUN AND EARTH

HOW LONG IT TAKES
one hour

WHAT YOU NEED
12-inch (30-cm) square of ⅛- to ¼-inch (.3- to .6-cm) plywood or thick, heavy cardboard
12-inch (30-cm) dowel ¼- to ⅜-inch (.6- to .9-cm) in diameter
thumbtacks
ruler
thin nail, at least one inch (2.5 cm) long
hammer
permanent marker
timer, alarm clock, or phone with alarm clock application
compass or phone with compass application
protractor
Internet access

What's a sundial? It's an ancient structure used to tell time. It uses an upright stick-shaped object to create a shadow on the ground allowing you to trace the sun's path.

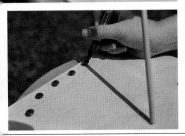

WHAT TO DO

1 USE THE RULER to find the center of your square on the back side.

2 FROM THE BACK side, use the hammer to push your nail all the way through.

3 SET THE END of the dowel on top of the nail point and hammer lightly to push it on top of the nail. This dowel is your gnomon—the upright object that will cast its shadow on your sundial.

4 USE THE INTERNET, a smartphone, or GPS to determine your latitude. This number will be the angle you need for your gnomon. For example, Bethel, Connecticut, is at 41° 37' 12° N, so we placed our gnomon at a 41° angle.

5 USE THE PROTRACTOR to find the angle for the gnomon. This will be your guide as you gently push the dowel over so that it is at the correct angle.

6 PLACE YOUR SUNDIAL on a stool in the middle of a sunny spot.

7 USE THE COMPASS to find north. Turn the sundial so that the gnomon lines up with the north-south direction.

8 CHECK THE TIME. At the top of each hour (8:00 a.m., say), check your sundial. Keeping the gnomon pointed north, trace the sun's shadow of the gnomon, and push a thumbtack in at the end of the shadow, or along it. Use a permanent marker to write the time on the thumbtack. With a ruler and the marker, trace the path of the shadow from the thumbtack to the gnomon at the center of the square.

9 SET THE ALARM for one hour ahead, and push in another thumbtack for the shadow of the gnomon at that time.

10 ONCE EVERY HOUR of the day—the time when the sun is up—repeat this, until you have a dial half full of thumbtacks. (The other half of the dial is night!)

11 AFTER YOU have finished marking each hour, you'll be able to check the sundial to see what time it is.

WHAT TO EXPECT Sundial shadows will be shortest when the sun is directly overhead, and long to the point where they extend off the sundial in morning and evening.

WHAT'S GOING ON? As the Earth revolves, the angle of the sun shining on any point changes. You can make a basic sundial out of any upright (from a pencil to a building) and some kind of markers (from a pencil mark to a giant stone) to show the path the upright's shadow takes as the angle of the sun changes.

QUESTION THIS!

• Check your sundial at the same time on other days. Do the markings and times match up?

• Is a sundial a good way to tell the time?

• Can you explain how the sun moves as it does?

• How effective are sundials during daylight saving time?

BRUSHY-BOTS

Old brushes . . . new motion, new action, new use!

CONCEPTS

ELECTRICITY, MOTOR, ENGINEERING, MOTION DYNAMICS

>> **HOW LONG IT TAKES**
one hour

WHAT YOU NEED
for each brushybot:
a used toothbrush, nail brush, or hairbrush
foam tape
scissors or wire cutters
watch battery
electrical tape
a motor of a size to power your brush

U se a little motor to power something that has legs made of brushes, wires, or anything else that moves when vibrated over a surface. Experimentation and invention is the name of the game here.

NOTE ABOUT MOTORS
If your motor doesn't have leads, you can solder copper or other wire onto it to act as leads, or use electrical tape to attach the head of a paper fastener. The leads, or legs of the paper fastener, are bent to connect with either side of the battery and power the motor.

1 USE SCISSORS or wire cutters to cut the handle off the toothbrush or hairbrush so you can use just the head (the bristle part). You don't need to cut anything off the fingernail brush.

2 CUT A PIECE of foam tape that will fit the back of the brush head. Stick it on.

3 YOUR MOTOR should have two wire leads sticking out of it, one black (positive) and one red (negative). Use a small square of electrical tape to affix the black (positive) wire lead to the battery.

4 STICK THE MOTOR onto the foam tape, being sure that the spinning weight on the motor has room to spin. You will need to let the weight hang off the end of the tape so that it can spin freely.

5 USE A SMALL SQUARE of electrical tape to hold the red (negative) wire lead onto the battery to make the connection and spin the motor, moving the brushybot.

6 OPTIONAL Stick a paper face on your robot for silliness or decorate it with googly eyes or whatever. I've seen dueling brushybots made with little warrior figures fighting each other. Why not?

WHAT TO EXPECT The motor will send vibrations to the bristles of the brush head, allowing it to move.

WHAT'S GOING ON? The motor will allow the brushybot to shake and shimmy in place or move in one direction or the other. If you create a paper track for it by turning up the edges of a stiff strip of paper, you can help channel the energy in one direction—and direct your brushybot. Angled bristles will change the motion of your brushybot.

GLITCH? Brush flips over when the motor starts? Connection shifts and motor stops? Move your components around, apply sticky foam or tape, add a dime to weigh things down. Again, experimentation and play are key here.

BONUS:
VIBRABOTS

Y ou can add wire legs to anything, stick a motor on top, and adjust it so it uses the motor's vibrations to move. Our vibrabots are a boxybot—a mint box carrying a motor, with wire legs and googly eyes; and a curlerbot—a hair curler with wire legs and a motor tucked inside. Our motors are weighted with pencil erasers.

OUR TRY

We used pager motors (small DC motors with an offset weight on the drive shaft) with leads to power our toothybots and fingernail brushybots, and larger motors (such as those from remote control airplanes) to power hairbrushybots, curlerbots, and boxybots. If you can, gather different size motors and different brushes and other items to try powering.

QUESTION THIS!

• Consider making two brushybots. Which brush head allows for a faster-moving brushybot?

• What other objects can you motorize this way?

MINI-SPINNERS

This top works on battery power.

> **HOW LONG IT TAKES**
> thirty minutes

> **WHAT YOU NEED**
> copper wire, 18 inches (45 cm) or more
> rechargeable or regular AA battery
> one to four neodymium (traditional) magnets
> pliers
> wire cutters

To complete the circuit and spin this spinner takes some trial and error (unless you have beginner's luck). The name of the game is tinkering: playing, adjusting, and revising until you get it going just right. Play until it works!

NOTE ABOUT MAGNETS These come in all sizes and widths. Cole used three dime-size magnets to power his spinner.

MINI-SPINNERS (CONTINUED)

WHAT TO DO

1 WRAP THE WIRE around the battery so that it forms a spiral or spring-shape, using four to six turns.

2 ATTACH THE MAGNETS to the bottom (negative terminal) of the battery, centering the battery.

3 YOUR GOAL is a coiled wire that circles the battery at the bottom, spirals up its length, and rests its tip on the top (positive node) of the battery. This should create the circuit you need to power the spinning motion.

a. At the bottom, coil the end of the wire tightly enough to fit when you set this coil over the battery and the magnet. You want the tail of the wire to fit around both when the battery is set on end atop the magnet, but the tail shouldn't rest on the table, instead hanging just above.

b. Twist and trim the top of the wire into a hook so that the end rests on the top of the battery.

c. Once you've got the shape and size of your coil right, take it off the battery. Use a paring knife or the edge of a coin to scrape the ends of the copper wire. Although you can't tell from looking at the wire, it is coated with insulation. To make the circuit work, you need to scrape this coating off. Scratch up the ends of the wire all the way around.

NOTE OF CAUTION
When you walk away from your spinner, take it apart. The battery can get hot, and you don't want that kind of trouble!

4 TEST YOUR MOTOR. Stand the flat end of the battery on the magnet and set the coil down over both. Adjust the top tail of the coil so that it touches the battery's top.

5 ADD AN OBJECT to the top of the coil. Some engineers have added copper wire hearts or dragonflies. Be creative! Attach this object to the top of the coil with wire, so that it spins when the coil turns.

WHAT TO EXPECT The wire, battery, and magnet should create a circuit and the coil will spin.

WHAT'S GOING ON? A homopolar motor is a simple motor with three components: a magnetic field, a conductor, and a battery. This spinner is a demonstration of the Lorentz Force, involving the force placed on a wire when it is placed in a magnetic field.

GLITCH? Your spinner just sits there, doing nothing—or the battery just gets hot and there's no action. For one thing, be aware that this circuit can sap the battery really quickly, so if you've been trying for a while without any spinning, consider swapping the battery for a fresh one. But honestly, this spinner can take a little bit of tinkering. Keep adjusting your wire so that the bottom touches the battery but the coil slides easily around the battery, and shift the top of the wire around until you feel the little buzz that tells you you've completed the circuit.

HUMAN SLINGSHOT

Remember the trouble we had with our lemon and potato batteries? (See pages 19–23.) Here's how we got rid of those failed batteries!

PROPULSION, ELASTICITY, ENGINEERING, DESIGN

HOW LONG IT TAKES
one hour

WHAT YOU NEED
an exercise band with handles
rubber bands
duct tape
the cap from a detergent bottle
some extra lemons and
potatoes (or similar biodegrad-
able items you have available)
optional: craft knife

HUMAN SLINGSHOT
(CONTINUED)

I f life gives you lemons—and potatoes—that won't light an LED, you can make lemonade. But we opted to find a creative way to get rid of our lemons.

WHAT TO DO

1 FIND THE CENTER of your exercise band.

2 USE THE RUBBER BANDS to attach the detergent bottle cap to the center of the exercise band, and duct tape it firmly around the rubber bands. Your goal is to affix the cap solidly enough that it will not fly off when you "fire" the slingshot.

3 EXPERIMENT to find a stance and method for firing the slingshot—which should be about the same length as your height when it is stretched out.

> GLITCH? The cap falls off when you fire it? The lemon or potato sticks in the cup and doesn't go anywhere? The answer is to tinker.

OUR TRY

This slingshot was our invention, and it took some trial and error to put it together and figure out the best way to fire it. Our design was the result of several false starts. The hardest part was figuring out what kind of saddle or cup we could use to hold the lemons and potatoes. We tried socks, fabric, and a kind of saddle made by braiding three exercise bands together. None of these gave enough spring—or they wouldn't release the lemon or potato. Paper and plastic cups tore. In the end, we looked for a rigid plastic cup that wouldn't change its shape and could just ride on the elastic without being pulled apart or stretched. The answer was the cap to a detergent bottle.

But how to attach the cap to the elastic? We found that a combination of rubber bands and duct tape did the trick without keeping the elastic from stretching, so it could fire. We used a craft knife to trim the rim off the cap so it wouldn't get caught on the elastic.

Then we experimented with methods for firing the slingshot. Sossi tried lying flat on the ground and sitting. Trijon tried standing up and pulling back. In the end our best shots came two ways:

One-person method: Sossi put her feet in the handles, lay back on a lounge chair, loaded the cap, and pulled the slingshot back by pulling her hands up to her shoulders, then releasing it.

Three-person method: Ariel and Sossi held the slingshot handles, while Trijon loaded the cup, pulled it back, and let the lemon fly. Goodbye, lemons. They're gone, thanks to another great try!

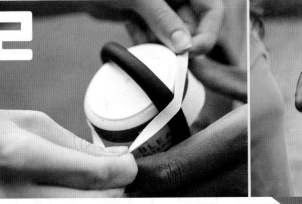

TRY THIS! AT THE SCIENCE FAIR

THE QUESTION

Not everything can be shaped into a science fair project, but most things can—if they include a phenomenon that can be observed given the right conditions.

SOME PHENOMENA IN THIS BOOK

IF CHICKEN SOUP IS LEFT IN A WARM PLACE FOR FOUR DAYS, A BIOFILM MAY FORM ON THE INSIDE OF THE CONTAINER. (Page 40)

IF I PLACE TWO TREATS ON THE FLOOR AND POINT TO ONE, MY DOG MAY GO TO THE TREAT I POINT TO. (Page 56)

IF I MIX BAKING SODA AND VINEGAR IN A GLASS, THE REACTION MAY BE ABLE TO PRODUCE GAS THAT INFLATES A GLOVE. (Page 88)

So, what can you do with each of these phenomena to make them into science fair projects?

Ask yourself a few questions:

WHAT ARE THE CONDITIONS INVOLVED IN THIS PHENOMENON?

WHAT CAN BE TESTED, CHANGED, OR COMPARED?

For example, in the first phenomenon, the one about the biofilm, the room is warm.

You could try doing the experiment at different temperatures to see what works. Here are a few more questions to shape the experiment in different ways.

Science Fair Question:
At what temperature will biofilm grow best?

Science Fair Question:
What medium (soup or other liquid) works best for growing biofilm?

Science Fair Question:
What works best as a medium for growing biofilm: low-sodium chicken soup or regular chicken soup?

THE EXPERIMENT

Once you have narrowed down your topic and come up with your question, consider what you could do as an experiment. Here are the pieces of the experiment that you need to have in place for the science fair.

> HYPOTHESIS: What you think will happen.

For example, your hypothesis could be that it won't make any difference if the soup is low-sodium or regular chicken soup.

> BACKGROUND RESEARCH: Information about your topic that would be good to know before you start, or that you need to find as you go along.

For example, you might do more research about biofilm and how it forms in the natural world (outside your science experiment, that is) and why it is an important subject for scientists to understand. You can start with the information in this book.

> MATERIALS: What you need to do your experiment.

For example: containers, soup, and so on. You can start with the project's materials list (WHAT YOU NEED) in this book.

> PROCEDURE: What you'll do for this experiment.

NOTE
Black light makes tonic water glow!

You may need to adapt the project in this book in order to narrow things down for your science fair project. For instance, how is the book project on biofilm different from the experiment we're proposing in which you compare low-sodium and regular chicken soup?

For instance, you're going to find out what works *better* as a growth medium for biofilm. How will you decide what *better* means in this situation? Do you mean *more* biofilm will grow? Or do you mean the biofilm *will grow faster*? Decide what you're going to measure, and come up with a way to measure it. Then plan your procedure, including the data you're gathering.

Say you find that biofilm grows really fast in low-sodium chicken soup in a warm room, and slower in regular chicken soup in a cold room. You may realize that low-sodium soup is a good medium . . . or is it warm soup that's a good medium? *Hmm.*

For instance, you may realize that you don't know enough about the conditions in which biofilm grows to make a firm conclusion. Oops. Is it a big mistake to have compared two variables

at once? Looking ahead at a project in the way that we just have can help you weed out potential errors like this. Instead, you could decide to keep the soup at the same temperature, so that the only difference is the kind of soup—or try one kind of soup at different temperatures, so that the difference (the variable) is the temperature. In this case, you could make things more interesting by adding another kind of soup or a different temperature reading.

But most scientific papers by professional scientists do end with a statement about what needs to be researched next. Your project should end with a question or comment about how you could learn more.

The next few pages include some things you're going to need to present to your teacher and/or science fair committee and some advice on how to make them shine.

TIP

Consider your project backward. You know what your experiment is going to be, and you know you're going to need a demonstration and/or poster and presentation. What parts will you need to complete? Before you start, plan on filling in the blanks by looking for exactly what you need as you work forward. For example, if you think your science fair booth would be stronger if you included a diagram of your experiment, plan on drawing one in your lab notes before you begin.

TRY THIS!

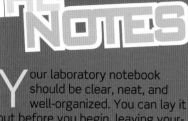

THE NOTES

Your laboratory notebook should be clear, neat, and well-organized. You can lay it out before you begin, leaving yourself extra space for each area you want to complete.

> Number the pages, and date each page as you work on your project.

In your book, list the goals of your project and the different jobs you have to do to complete it. Then break down each job into steps, and document (take notes on) what you do as you complete each step. Add drawings and photographs, and keep note of materials and procedures you used. You might think this is silly, since you're the one doing things, following directions carefully. But if you note each thing you're doing, the date and time you do it, and what you find at each step, this will translate easily into your write-up and presentations. It will make it easier for you to remember not only what you did and when you did it, but what you felt and thought as you went along.

> Organize your data-gathering in tables and charts.

Say you are testing three subjects to see how they respond to your variables. For example, you are doing leaf chromatography (page 17) on three leaves. For each leaf,

make a table showing where the leaf was gathered, how long it was tested, and the pigments that you found. As you go through the process of the experiment, all you'll have to do is fill in the blanks in your table. Simple!

In your notes, include what you think about the data and whether they reflect your expectations before you started.

> Keep note of mistakes or complications or problems that arise as you work.

Include these issues in your write-up as you explain the situations that may have affected your results. If possible, repeat your experiment to see if you can amend the situation, but include the first trials in your report.

THE WRITE-UP

One-third of most science fair grades will come from the paper, write-up, or report you write about your experiment or project.

CONSIDER YOUR EXPERIENCE and create a
project title. This can be a word, phrase, or question that shows what you learned from your experience or shows what you were curious about when you started.

BEGIN with an abstract, a brief
description of the project and summary of your experiment and findings. An abstract is like a trailer for a film: It tells people about the project and makes them want to know more.

CREATE a table of contents
that reflects the pieces of your project. (This will help you structure your paper. Plan the parts of your paper first, then just fill in what is needed.)

WRITE your introduction to give
the purpose of your work. (Why did you choose this project?) State what you hoped to discover and give your hypothesis.

TELL about the research you did
to find out more about your topic, procedure, method, and materials. The review of literature is where to put information about others who have worked on your question, what they learned or did, and how their work relates to yours.

DESCRIBE your process. List
and describe your materials, the steps in your procedure, and your results. This may be the longest part of your paper, written in careful detail so that another scientist could follow your process the way a cook follows a recipe.

SHOW your raw data—the mea-
surements or other numbers—just as you found them. You may include excerpts from your notes, including tables and calculations.

ORGANIZE your data. Add
tables or graphs that make it easy to see what your data told you. Use Microsoft Excel or another graphing program.

WRITE your conclusion. This tells
what you found out by doing your experiment. Circle back to your hypothesis, and discuss whether the result of your experiment agreed with your hypothesis.

SYNTHESIZE future indica-
tions. State the questions your work raised. Talk about future experiments that might be—or must be—done before this subject can be fully understood.

LIST your sources. Create a clear
and specific bibliography or "works cited" page.

THE BOOTH

What's in your booth? Here's another planning backward tip: Think about what you'll want to talk about and show people as you stand in your booth at the science fair.

THE TABLE: Try to include things—besides your poster or display board—that help a viewer "see" your lab. Include your laboratory notebook and some of your materials. If it's possible to share some of the procedures or findings in physical form at your table, do so.

THE DEMONSTRATION: You can't often replicate your whole experiment in your science fair booth, but you may be able to show some aspect of it. For example, you could have containers on display with biofilm growing in several stages. Or how about some biofilm under a dissecting microscope for visitors to view? This helps bring your experiment to life.

POSTER TIPS

Use a headline and smaller subheads to chunk up your information. This allows a viewer to scan your poster and easily see what your project is about without having to read every detail.

Use a big font so it can be read at a distance.

Plan your visuals so that they, too, can be easily scanned and understood. Include captions.

Consider what's the most important thing you want people to understand as they look at your poster.

NOTE ON SCIENCE FAIR JUDGES
There's no guarantee the president will show up to talk to you at your booth, but you should prepare as if he will!

POSTER OR DISPLAY BOARD:

Scientists create these to help them show their work. Check the Internet for sample scientific posters and prize-winning science fair display boards. Your science poster gives a short-form version of your paper, write-up, or report, including:

- project title
- abstract
- question (the question the experiment was designed to answer)
- hypothesis
- background research
- materials
- procedure
- results
- conclusion
- future indications or questions

TALKING TO JUDGES AND OTHER VISITORS:

Plan what to say and how to say it. What's the most important point that you want to make when people ask you to tell them about your project? Know what information you want them to walk away with when they leave your booth.

Introduce yourself, giving your name loud and clear. Go on to give the name of your project and tell the subject of it. Tell what it was you wanted to find out and describe what you did in order to accomplish that. Then describe the data you gathered and explain what it told you about your topic. Finally, add a statement about what else you'd like to find out or what you want people to consider. Thank your listeners for their time and take questions.

TALKING TIPS

Rehearse and time your statement and be ready to give it. Cut it if it's too long.

Ask someone to help you guess what kinds of questions you might be asked so that you can plan how to answer them.

STEM

SCIENCE STANDARDS

To align with Science, Technology, Engineering, Math (STEM), each experiment in this book has been correlated with the Next Generation Science Standards (NGSS), which are based on the Framework for K-12 Science Education developed by the National Research Council. Below you will find a list of each experiment in this book along with the standards they align to. At the end of each standard description you'll notice a number and some letters. These represent the grade level, subject area, and standard number for each standard (example: 4-LS1-1 represents a fourth grade standard, in life, physical, or earth and space science, standard number one). For more details on NGSS, visit www.nextgenscience.org.

RAINBOW ROSE, Page 10

Standard(s)

Construct an argument that plants and animals have internal and external structures that function to support survival, growth, behavior, and reproduction. (4-LS1-1)

Conduct an investigation to provide evidence that living things are made of cells; either one cell or many different numbers and types of cells. (MS-LS1-1)

SEED BOMBS AND SLINGSHOTS, Page 12

Standard(s)

Use evidence to support the explanation that traits can be influenced by the environment. (3-LS3-2)

Construct a scientific explanation based on evidence for how environmental and genetic factors influence the growth of organisms. (MS-LS1-5)

CABBAGE CHECK, Page 15

Standard(s)

Make observations and measurements to identify materials based on their properties. (5-PS1-3)

LEAF CHROMATOGRAPHY, Page 17

Standard(s)

Make observations and measurements to identify materials based on their properties. (5-PS1-3)

LEMON-LIT AND POTATO-POWERED LED, Page 19

Standard(s)

Apply scientific ideas to design, test, and refine a device that converts energy from one form to another. (4-PS3-4)

Develop and use a model to describe that waves are reflected, absorbed, or transmitted through various materials. (MS-PS4-2)

SEEDS SPROUT IN WATER BEADS, Page 24

Standard(s)

Develop models to describe that organisms have unique and diverse life cycles but all have in common birth, growth, reproduction, and death. (3-LS1-1)

Support an argument that plants get the materials they need for growth chiefly from air and water. (5-LS1-1)

BUG AMBULANCE, Page 28

Standard(s)

Construct an argument that plants and animals have internal and external structures that function to support survival, growth, behavior, and reproduction. (4-LS1-1)

CRICKET TRAINING, Page 30

Standard(s)

Use a model to describe that animals receive different types of information through their senses, process the information in their brain, and respond to the information in different ways. (4-LS1-2)

Gather and synthesize information that sensory receptors respond to stimuli by sending messages to the brain for immediate behavior or storage as memories. (MS-LS1-8)

WHAT COLORS DO BUTTERFLIES LIKE?, Page 32

Standard(s)

Use a model to describe that animals receive different types of information through their senses, process the information in their brain, and respond to the information in different ways. (4-LS1-2)

Gather and synthesize information that sensory receptors respond to stimuli by sending messages to the brain for immediate behavior or storage as memories. (MS-LS1-8)

YEAST COLONY, Page 35

Standard(s)

Use evidence to support the explanation that traits can be influenced by the environment. (3-LS3-2)

WHAT DIED?, Page 38

Standard(s)

Develop a model to describe the movement of matter among plants, animals, decomposers, and the environment. (5-LS2-1)

Develop a model to describe the cycling of matter and flow of energy among living and nonliving parts of an ecosystem. (MS-LS2-3)

GROW YOUR OWN BIOFILM, Page 40

Standard(s)

Construct a scientific explanation based on evidence for how environmental and genetic factors influence the growth of organisms. (MS-LS1-5)

HULA-HOOP OBSERVATION, Page 42

Standard(s)

Plan an investigation to provide evidence that the change in an object's motion depends on the sum of the forces on the object and the mass of the object. (MS-PS2-2)

PHONY SMILES, Page 48

Standard(s)

Use a model to describe that animals receive different types of information through their senses, process the information in their brain, and respond to the information in different ways. (4-LS1-2)

SORTING THE TRASH, Page 50

Standard(s)

Apply scientific principles to design a method for monitoring and minimizing a human impact on the environment. (MS-ESS3-3)

Apply Newton's Third Law to design a solution to a problem involving the motion of two colliding objects. (MS-PS2-1)

RIGHTY LEFTY, Page 52

Standard(s)

Analyze and interpret data to provide evidence that plants and animals have traits inherited from parents and that variation of these traits exists in a group of similar organisms. (3-LS1-1)

Use a model to describe that animals receive different types of information through their senses, process the information in their brain, and respond to the information in different ways. (4-LS1-2)

DOG BED SOCK I.D., Page 54

Standard(s)

Gather and synthesize information that sensory receptors respond to stimuli by sending messages to the brain for immediate behavior or storage as memories. (MS-LS1-8)

DOGS AND POINTING, Page 56

Standard(s)

Use a model to describe that animals receive different types of information through their senses, process the information in their brain, and respond to the information in different ways. (4-LS1-2)

Gather and synthesize information that sensory receptors respond to stimuli by sending messages to the brain for

immediate behavior or storage as memories. (MS-LS1-8)

CAT IQ TEST, Page 58

Standard(s)

Use a model to describe that animals receive different types of information through their senses, process the information in their brain, and respond to the information in different ways. (4-LS1-2)

EGG TRICK #1, Page 60

Standard(s)

Analyze and interpret data on the properties of substances before and after the substances interact to determine if a chemical reaction has occurred. (MS-PS1-2)

MAKE FOOTPRINT CASTS, Page 63

Standard(s)

Analyze and interpret data to provide evidence that plants and animals have traits inherited from parents and that variation of these traits exists in a group of similar organisms. (3-LS3-1)

NEARSIGHTED HOOPS, Page 66

Standard(s)

Use evidence to support the explanation that traits can be influenced by the environment. (3-LS3-2)

LIGHT-UP ICE BALL, Page 70

Standard(s)

Apply scientific ideas to design, test, and refine a device that converts energy from one form to another. (4-PS3-4)

Develop and use a model to describe that waves are reflected, absorbed, or transmitted through various materials. (MS-PS4-2)

STEM

INDEX

ACKNOWLEDGMENTS

F. Todd Baker, Emeritus Professor of Physics,
University of Georgia
askthephysicist.com

Bethel BMXers, especially Garrett
Bethel Cycle Shop
Jen Matlack
Parloa Park
Maryclaire and Douglas Quine

Emily F. Young

All photographs shot on location by
Matthew Rakola unless otherwise
noted below:

Cover, 2 (girl), Avesun/Shutterstock;
148, Molly Riley-Pool/Getty Images;
149, Parveen Negi/India Today Group/
Getty Images; 158, courtesy of the
author

OUR MODELS

Humans:

Aaliyah	Dylan	Marco
Abigail	Emily	Nick
Adriana	Isaac	Nikitha
Allison	Janelle	Niyanna
Ariel	Jarrett	Patsy
Bailey	Jason	Priyanka
Brandon	Jen	Serenity
Caitlyn	Justin	Sossi
Cole	Lori	Stephanie
Doug	Luke	Trijon
	Mae	Wyatt

Special thanks to
Tina Kiniry at the
John Casablancas
Modeling Agency

Jen's and Mae's cats:
Jack
Olive

Karen's cat:
Taegu

Karen's dogs:
Cherubino
Rosamund

Michael's dog:
Truffles

Others:
bees
beetles
biofilm
crayfish
crickets
dragonflies
flies/maggots
microbes
slugs
spiders
yeast

RESOURCES/SHOPPING TIPS/NOTES

For specific supplies, here are some national chain and Internet sources. You should be able to find most of them at local independent stores, too.

1 Rainbow Rose

Wilton's food coloring. Michaels

2 Seed Bombs and Slingshot

Crayola air-dry clay. Target
Surgical tubing. Lowe's

5 Potato-Powered LEDs and Lemon-Lit LEDs

2.5 volt LEDs. Radio Shack (online)
Test leads. Sparkfun.com

6 Seeds Sprout in Water Beads

Water gems. Michaels
Orbeez. Amazon

7 Bug Ambulance

Bug vacuum anteater. Uncle Milton's/ National Geographic

8 Cricket Training

Bug Box Crickets. Choice Pet Supply

10 Yeast Colony

Agar petri dishes. Carolina Biological Supply

13 Hula-Hoop Observation

Tubing, connectors, pipe cutter. Lowe's

23 Light-Up Ice Ball

LED, battery casing, AA battery. Radio Shack

24 Highlighted Water

Black light, 18". Spencer's
Tide detergent. Target

26 Water Beads

Water beads: Water Gems, Michaels

30 Ghost Glove

Surgical gloves. CVS. Or you can ask your doctor or dentist to give you one or two. (My dentist did.)

37 MYO Giant Air Cannon

Bonus: Smoke Rings
Color smoke balls. Amazon

38 and 39 Bike Wheel Gyroscope #1 and #2

BMX foot pegs and wheels. Amazon

43 Ice-Skater Effect

Hand weights. Target

47 Make a Sundial

Wooden disks. Michaels

48 Brushybots

Pager motors, 1.5-3-volt DC motors, battery leads. Radio Shack (online)

49 Mini-Spinners

Neodymium magnets. K & J Magnetic (online)

50 Human Slingshot

Exercise bands. Target

CREDITS

Published by the National Geographic Society

John M. Fahey, *Chairman of the Board and Chief Executive
Officer*
Declan Moore, *Executive Vice President; President,
Publishing and Travel*
Melina Gerosa Bellows, *Executive Vice President; Chief
Creative Officer, Books, Kids, and Family*

Prepared by the Book Division

Hector Sierra, *Senior Vice President and General Manager*
Nancy Laties Feresten, *Senior Vice President, Kids
Publishing and Media*
Jennifer Emmett, *Vice President, Editorial Director,
Kids Books*
Eva Absher-Schantz, *Design Director, Kids Publishing
and Media*
Jay Sumner, *Director of Photography, Kids Publishing
and Media*
R. Gary Colbert, *Production Director*
Jennifer A. Thornton, *Director of Managing Editorial*

Staff for This Book

Priyanka Lamichhane, *Project Editor*
Eva Absher-Schantz, *Art Director*
Lori Epstein, *Senior Photo Editor*
Itzhack Shelomi, *Designer*
Ariane Szu-Tu, *Editorial Assistant*
Paige Towler, *Editorial Intern*
Callie Broaddus, *Design Production Assistant*
Margaret Leist, *Photo Assistant*
Grace Hill, *Associate Managing Editor*
Joan Gossett, *Production Editor*
Lewis R. Bassford, *Production Manager*
Susan Borke, *Legal and Business Affairs*

Production Services

Phillip L. Schlosser, *Senior Vice President*
Chris Brown, *Vice President, NG Book Manufacturing*
George Bounelis, *Senior Production Manager*
Nicole Elliott, *Director of Production*
Rachel Faulise, *Manager*
Robert L. Barr, *Manager*

Trade paperback edition ISBN: 978-1-4263-1711-8
Library edition ISBN: 978-1-4263-1712-5

Printed in Hong Kong
14/THK/1